EXPOSED

EXPOSED

The naked Uncensored Truth
to Running A Successful
Photography Business

Robert Provencher

ANDBOROUGH
PUBLISHING

Andborough Publishing
4935 Sprangler Drive
Colorado Springs, Colorado 80922
USA

Exposed: The Naked Uncensored Truth to Running a Successful Photography Business
Copyright© 2006 & 2007 Robert Provencher

First Printing November 2006
Second Printing March 2007 (Revised)

Disclaimer and/or Legal Notices:
While all attempts have been made to verify information in this publication, the author does not assume any responsibility for errors, inaccuracies or omissions.

This publication is not intended for use as a source of legal or accounting advice. The purchaser or reader of this publication assumes responsibility for the use of these materials the information herein. The author and publisher assumes no responsibility or liability whatsoever on the behalf of the purchaser or reader.

Publishers Cataloging-in-Publication Data

Provencher, Robert 1958-
    Exposed: The naked uncensored truth to running a successful photography
    business/Robert Provencher.—Rev. ed.
      p.cm
    Includes bibliographical references and index
    ISBN - 13 978-0-9774181-4-5
    ISBN - 10 0-9774181-4-6
    1. Photography—Marketing.   2. Photography—Business methods.   3. Commercial
    photography.   I. Title.

Library of Congress Control Number: 2007900906

Printed in the United States of America

Dedication

To my Mom & Dad,
who made me and always believed in me.

To my four sisters,
The first "hot babes" I ever photographed.

To my loving wife, Tina,
without her, success wouldn't be possible.

To my beautiful daughter Danielle,
who I love more than a million red skittles.

To James Hodgins, my bestest student, who now inspires and
teaches me, and his success is a living testament since his
eagerness to grow and listen (most of the time) paved the way.

To all my friends,
without friends there would be nothing.

To my old girlfriend Jennifer's mom,
who said about my career, 'that's no way to make a living!'

And to all the members at
No Bs Photo Success.

When you grow, I grow.

Contents

EXPOSED

Contents

Contents

EXPOSED

Contents

A Note From Rob

Who in their right mind would put a bare, butt-naked photo of themselves on the cover of their book? That's me. Nobody ever said I was normal.

This book is the truth about success in the running of a portrait studio and the way I see it. You may not agree with any or all of it. If my job were to be agreeable, I wouldn't 'expose' myself so much. Nor would my book contain what I see as valuable insights and information. If any, or worse yet, all of it peeves you off, I make no apologies.

I can only hope that you don't walk from this book feeling angry. That would be an awful waste of your time. At least try to get something of value.

Having said that, it is my sincerest belief that most of what you will read in these pages will be very interesting and valuable to you. I feel most will walk away with that impression. The few who don't may end up, as is the rule, making the most noise.

If you were to ask me for a simple solution to success, in as few words as is possible, here it is: create a vision and work your butt off. There is no more to it. However, work smart, do something you love, and make tons of money in as short a time as you can.

Good luck and good reading,
Robert Provencher

"This is the true joy in life...being used for a purpose recognized by yourself as a mighty one...being a force of Nature instead of a feverish selfish little clod of ailments and grievances complaining that the world will not devote itself to making you happy...I am of the opinion that my life belongs to the whole community and as long as I live it is my privilege to do for it whatever I can.

I want to be used up when I die. For the harder I work the more I live. I rejoice in life for its own sake. Life is no brief candle to me. It's a sort of splendid torch which I've got to hold up for the moment and I want to make it burn as brightly as possible before handing it on to future generations."

- George Bernard Shaw, 1856-1950
(Playwrite, Nobel Prize awardee
and Oscar winner)

Introduction

This is everything I know about photography and running a photography studio, based on 27 years of playing the game.

There's an inner voice inside me that nags me and asks, "Who are you? Who are you to write a book on this topic? Who are you to write a book on photography and not include any photographs?"

It's kind of crazy when you think about it. Right?

All great deeds, all great ventures, all businesses, pretty much anything that we produce in our lives, are all based on and initially start from an idea. Ideas are where it's at. Ideas are very cool.

I hope this book will be just that for you – an idea, or a series of ideas, that will inspire you because you have read my history, my story, and my observations and thoughts that I've collected over the years.

As a child in school, I was very much asleep and in la-la land most of the time. For me, school was dream time. And as a result, I wasn't the class clown. I was very shy. I became very much a wallflower, kind of invisible. There observing half the time and half the time in dream land.

This is important to note because it sort of molded me in many ways. I'm a big believer in taking everything that we've become in our lives and turning them into strengths – into things that we can use in a positive way – because all too often we get caught up in the negative side of things.

For photographers, we can take whatever we are, or whatever neurotic impulses we've developed over the years, we could take whatever things we can perceive as being very negative and turn them into very positive things. And we can massage these things, these characteristics, these aspects of our personality, and we can bring them forward and develop a strong talent. We can develop and encourage our creative sides.

THE BIZ

Of course, let's not forget about the business side. In this book I'm going to get into the business side of things. I'm going to get into marketing. I'm going to get into the creative side of photography as well, because I believe that in order to be successful you have to have all of these elements working together.

Like I always say in my coaching program, and like I nag and constantly bring up, over and over and over again, everything starts with the individual. And this book is about an individual – it's about me.

And you. Really, I'm exposing everything. I'm telling you, giving you everything I can possibly come up with that I've observed from being in the back of the room, the shy kid in school, the guy who barely talked; now you can't shut me up.

But here I am saying it the way I see it. You may not agree with some of it. You may not agree with all of it. Hopefully, at the very least, you come away with some new ideas. You come away with some new concepts that will inspire you to become a better photographer, a better businessman, and a better marketer.

I wrote this essentially for photographers, but for photographers of a certain breed . . . the ones who are always looking and learning, and wanting to find newer and better ways to create a stronger business, to create a better product, namely their photography, and to create a more fulfilling life through their photography businesses.

BEING AN IDEA MACHINE

There's a book that I read years ago. I guess I was about twenty years old. And I don't even remember the guy's name. I know his first name is Robin, and it was called Creative Photography. That's all the title was.

There wasn't a single picture in that book. But I always remembered it. And I read it several times, because the ideas in it somehow worked for me. Now this guy was a stock photographer. I am not a stock photographer; I'm a wedding and portrait photographer. Nevertheless, the ideas helped me. Helped in some way develop who I eventually became and who I am still becoming.

So again, I'd like to reiterate that fact that ideas are where it's at. Hopefully you get the ideas in this book. Read them. Try and follow them as best you can, and understand them. Keep an open mind. If you have any thoughts or feedback or concepts that you would like to make me aware of or debate, whatever, I'm easy. You can always contact me or send me an email.

THE CREATIVE FACTOR

A few thoughts on creativity. Creativity is a part of this whole process; creativity insofar as innovation in business and as in our abilities to create photographs.

But, there are two sides to the creativity coin. When you look at the whole picture, there are more dimensions than just being an artist. Because, as photographers we tend to get stuck in ruts, we tend to find a system that works, and we get into that system and we stick with it – forever. After decades of using the same system over and over and over, we end up calcifying and submitting what worked for us the first time. That's great. Maybe.

The problem is, you want to avoid obsolescence. Because if what you're doing does become obsolete, you may have a struggle. You may have a hard time breaking away from it and creating a new system.

The idea that I like to express to you is that, we need to learn as many variations on as many aspects as is completely possible in our business, in our photography, so that we can keep an open mind, and we can learn to innovate at both levels, as photographers and as business persons.

This is vital. Part of becoming a complete, wholesome, prosperous, excited and growing photographer is exploring the many dimensions and areas for growth and opportunity in business and in creativity.

School is never out for the pro.

EXPOSED

The naked Uncensored Truth
to Running A Successful
Photography Business

CHAPTER 1

Photography is Business

"Talent is cheaper than table salt. What separates the talent-ed individual from the successful one is a lot of hard work."

- Stephen King
(American Author)

P eople ask me, "What does it take to be successful in photogra-phy?" I think many people have an oversimplified idea, or they have thoughts about photography that are impressed upon them from and within our culture and from movies, and just vague impres-sions that they've had, which then ultimately ends up being oversim-plified. Even photographers who have many years experience often-times have a skewed impression and realization of what it takes to be successful in photography. I'd like to clear that up once and for all.

A PASSIONATE PROFESSION

My answer to everybody who asks the question, 'what does it take to be a good photographer or to succeed in photography?' is: passion. It's a one-word answer – passion. All you need is passion.

To be fair, we should look at that word and look at the field of pho-tography a little bit deeper, by looking at the business side. Because when you balance your passion with the business side, and you end up profiting from your talents and running a successful business, it's a re-ally good thing.

You end up with prosperity, as well as the ability to create images on an ongoing basis. To me, this is the ultimate state. It's energizing! It's invigorating! It's exciting! But it's not easy for most of us, or for many of us.

I got into photography probably for the same reason that you and a lot of other people got into photography – because they felt very passionate about it. And, because of the babes. When I was in college at the young age of 19, I first discovered photography simply because it was one of the courses that I was taking.

I had no idea what was about to happen to me.

I had no idea that I was going to become so hooked and overwhelmed and driven by this passion and desire for this media. I look back, and I look at that initial experience, and how it set the stage for what was to become, and what still is a life-long ambition – that was well over 25 years ago.

I have heard many stories from other photographers who have had similar experiences. But I also heard from many other photographers' experiences that miss out a very important element. This is the side of photography that is often ignored, overlooked, or not given its due attention – and that is the business side.

Photography is a business. Obviously, if you want to earn an income and you want to earn a respectable income doing something that you love, you have to approach the business side very, very seriously. But you must strive for balance – balance in business and balance in photography.

When I first discovered the importance of business and marketing, and when I started to apply certain fundamental truths about business and in marketing, my photography studio really began to flourish. I always did fairly well, considering all things. But I did exceptionally well, once I got serious about the business side.

A UNIQUE CAREER CHOICE

One thing that I like about photography and the field of portrait photography is that it's not like many other career choices. A lot of career choices are intangibles, like accounting or law or financial planning. These fields are more based on abstract concepts. These fields are intangible. In photography, you get to create on an ongoing basis. I think that's so cool. Every day, every week, every month, year by year, I get to create, literally, thousands of images. Not only that, I get to create images that impact people's lives. Hundreds and thousands of people are affected by the images that I create. And I also get to create a good living from it.

Is it a respectable career? Absolutely. When you achieve this state, it is, in my opinion, at least as respectable or more than most careers out there, but also for the sole purpose that it is my career. It is my career choice. And when I first started out, I was given stern warnings about the difficulties that lay ahead. I was 19 years old when I decided that I wanted to pursue a career in photography. I'd only known photography for approximately four months. I had very little schooling. To be fair, you can consider me a college dropout, twice.

But I've managed to create a respectable career, which also indicates that a formal education is not a prerequisite in this career choice. As a matter of fact, just like I spoke of earlier, you can use your passion. And if you combine it properly with the business side, you can create a very respectable career. But, it's not easy. Like I said, I was given stern warnings about how difficult the road was to be, and from very reliable sources. And those warnings were very accurate, as I soon discovered.

When I got into photography throughout my early 20s and onwards, I struggled quite a bit. But I also, at the same time, had a continuous drive and ambition. To me, it was a given that I was going to be self-employed. I guess given the fact that my father and all his brothers and my grandfather, and all my uncles were self-employed. So when I grew up, being self-employed was just something that you did. It wasn't something that was unusual. So going after a 9 to 5, safe and secure job was a bit of an alien concept for me. So getting into photography and taking steps towards the business side was as natural as breeding.

In spite of that, I still had a lot of innocence, and I was still extremely naïve in many ways. So, I had to discover and look into the deeper sides of what it took to really succeed. This took quite a while for me. Hopefully for you, you can take a few shortcuts. Hopefully, once you've established yourself as a talented photographer, you can apply some of the business principles and some of the marketing strategies that I've laid out in this book. You can "leapfrog" ahead. Nothing says that you have to take a certain amount of time to become sanctioned or qualified to "earn your dues." You can take as little time as is required to achieve the goals in this field that you wish to. The only thing stopping you is your ability to create a good product, or in other words, your talents. Beyond that, the only thing stopping you would be any limitations you have in your own mind.

One thing I like about this career is, hey, I get to sleep in. It's wonderful. I don't have to get up at six in the morning and be at some workplace for seven, eight in the morning. That suits me just fine because it's my character. Although, I find that, as I get older, I've been waking up earlier. Generally speaking, I've always been a night owl. And I notice that about a few friends of mine, who are very successful photographers, they're the same way. They often will work until past midnight and sleep in a little bit. In many ways, it's not really work. It's fun. I have a great time doing this and making money at it. It's a lifestyle choice. Photography is a great choice that suits a lifestyle for certain personalities. And I like to think that I fit that personality.

THE ARTIST WITHIN

There's a bit of a bohemian side to it – a bit of the artistic side to it. But we must never forget the business side. There are many side issues that spring up as a result of a limiting thought process that comes from thinking that we are artists, and that we must have certain elements that are artistic. We must abide by these artistic rules. Some people even manage to get a little bit confused about the importance of earning money and a profit through their artistic endeavours. Or, they somehow think that because they're an artist, they have to suffer – art is suffering. Nothing could be further from the truth.

When you look through the history of art when you go back hundreds of years, oil painting used to be the popular medium. And Rembrandt, as well as other famous artists, used to earn a profit from their endeavours. Rembrandt had literally a factory, where he had people who were being trained in the ways of the craft, and he would mass-produce paintings for sale. The whole purpose was to earn a profit. So I would like to say that he had a pretty good sense of what it took on the business side of things, in order to keep things going.

IGNORING THE GUILT

When you ignore the business side of things, you suffer and you put undue pressure on yourself. This actually affects your ultimate goal, which is to create nice photographs. So, it's an argument for learning how to make a profit and take care of business, and at the same time feel good about it. Get rid of the guilt. Get rid of the crappy feelings that often are associated with people who are in business, all the culturally influenced or all the false impressions that have been placed upon us from friends and family. We think that earning a profit is somehow bad, wrong, evil, and that as artists, it's not a good thing. You must adjust your own thinking in your own mind.

You must get it straight that earning a profit and running a successful business is very much a top priority. If you have any kind of mixed feelings, bad feelings or distorted feelings, as is so common with so many people, you must take that and look at it seriously, and create an image or at least a goal or a direction where you are going to start to get clear on this – where earning a profit is going to be something that you're very comfortable with.

Here's a side bonus: When you do become successful in business, you become a better 'artist'. The two are inextricably linked. Ignore this at your own peril.

CHAPTER 2

How to Really, Really, Really, Really Succeed in Your Own Photography Business

"Courage is the first of human qualities, because it is the quality which guarantees all others."

\- Sir Winston Churchill, 1874-1965
(English statesman, soldier, author and former
Prime Minister of the United Kingdom)

Did you know the business statistics are very dismal? They're bleak at best, right across the board for most businesses. Photography studios fare no better, probably even worse. Let's look at those statistics for a second.

The fact is that 80 percent of businesses in the first five years some say as high as 90 percent fail. They pack it in. After the first five years, another 80 percent, some say 90 percent, during the next five years, fail, too. When you look around you, you look at businesses opening up and closing their doors. It's no surprise. Most of them seem to last about a year. It's hard. Business is hard. It's not an easy thing. If it were real easy, we'd probably all be in business.

You know, there's a real love/hate relationship with most people who are not in business. They look at business owners and think to themselves, "Geez, I'd like to be in my own business." But they also at the same time seem to be, I don't know, filled with envy or jealousy, or anger, or they somehow think that business people are evil. So, it's not an easy thing that is easily laid out. It's not something you can just put a key in the door and open the door, and it's going to happen to you.

As a matter of fact, the real surprising thing to me was that most of what I discovered worked was stuff that kind of came up as it came up

– stuff that came after the fact. You don't know a lot of it until you get out there and start making it happen. You don't really know exactly what's going to create the sales, the phone calls, and the appointments. You have to modify it and improve upon it. Work with what works. Throw away what doesn't. This sometimes is hard for some people. It's called resiliency.

It's important to keep in mind that if you have a personality defect where you continuously keep banging your head against the wall trying stuff that doesn't work, it's not going to take you very long before you totally lose your mind and burnout. This is important.

RESILIENCE IS KEY

You have to be resilient. Resiliency is probably the number one key characteristic for most business owners. Once you become good at what it is you do, then you are prolific; then you are able to produce. And you want to get to that level as quickly as possible. As a photography studio owner, of course that means photographing sessions and making money off of each one of those sessions. In my marketing manuals that I've written over the years, the number one idea that I like to get across to people is that you must be a marketer of photographic goods – not a photographer. You must become a strategist, first and foremost. You must know how to strategize so that you create business on an ongoing, reliable basis, over and over, and over again.

The number one thing that I see happening for most photography studios is, "Well, I've got a camera. I've got some talent. I've got a sign, storefront, and a business card. That's all I need. Now, I deserve business." This is a really stupid way to think, act, and behave. Not only is it egotistical, narrow-minded and childish, but also, it is, in today's economy and today's day and age, a sure fire way to commit business suicide. You want to put your priorities in the right order. In my opinion marketing is number one; photography is number two.

BECOMING A GREAT MARKETER

Marketing is all about business. You want to get your business going, and the way you do that successfully is through marketing.

There are other ideas that you want to avoid, as well. One of which is throwing a lot of money at your business. That's a big mistake that a lot of first time business owners make. They have money available to them either through savings or mortgaging their homes or through some financial loan. They go in there, and they start throwing money at their business. In a matter of time, the money is all gone. I think it's very detrimental to have a lot of money. It's good to have money to buy equipment and have some leaseholds and have a car, but to throw money at a business and just to support the business month after month, it's only a matter of time before it's just going to quit. It's not going to work anymore. So this is important to understand.

So what is the solution, then, to becoming very effective as a marketer and to make the right decisions in business? In my opinion, start small, and build from there. Like I said in the last chapter, all businesses started at the kitchen table with a scratch pad, a pen, and a bunch of ideas. Start scratching out ideas. Start small, and you build. Now if you are going to get into a situation where you have an actual studio and you're going to invest in some bricks and mortar, you'd better have a good product. Your photography better be good enough; but that's not enough to get you going. If you do, it is by sheer luck and chance. And if you ever get caught in a situation where that's not going to count anymore, you better know what else needs to be done. So, you need a contingency plan. It's better to have a contingency plan now, as opposed to the future when you may need one. And that plan is to have some very powerful marketing and very strong, sound business principles working for you. Let's talk a little bit about those.

FOLLOWING SOUND BUSINESS PRINCIPLES

First of all, a business, in my opinion, is a reflection of the individual. Now I didn't create that idea. When I first read it, it was in the book by Paul Hawkens, Growing Your Business. When I read that, I just lit up. I knew it to be so true, and such a breath of fresh air to realize that hey, your business is you. It's your identity. It's who you are. So if your business turns to crap, well maybe your life has turned into crap. If your business fails, something you did is failing. So you have to take total responsibility – not blaming the economy, not blaming the strikes, not blaming your neighbours, your competition, your wife, your husband, your friends, your whatever. It's a reflection of you. So you have to be on the right path in order to start your business on the right path. This is essential. This is critical. This is do or die.

So look at yourself. Have a good, honest look at yourself. That's why I believe in improving on a continuous, ongoing basis, so that my business improves. You know, maybe I don't really want to improve, but I know that if I do, my business will improve. And it's not the only answer, but it is part of the big picture. Because if you have skeletons in your closet, it's only a matter of time before they come out and they start rattling around in every other aspect of your life and in your business. So you might as well take a good long, hard look at yourself and start your business on good solid footing – small steps, incrementally building your castle, one brick at a time.

If you have a lot of ambition, but you don't have a lot of savvy, or you're just not that bright in other areas, you must get bright. You must learn; develop the ability to learn how to make good, sound business decisions. If you don't have that ability, look for them. Ask other businesses; ask other people who are successful. Don't ask your friends or your neighbours who work at a 9 to 5 job. Don't ask your family who has nothing more than opinions. Go to people who are successful. You would be amazed at how helpful and useful most of these people are. It seems that the sounder they are, with their sound advice, the more eager they are. It's just that the people who are actually looking for this advice are far and few between. They more than welcome it, so you might as well knock on their doors and start asking questions. And if you find somebody who is totally resistant, don't go with that person. Maybe they're not the one. As a matter of fact, I can assure you that they are not the one.

Now what am I talking about here? I'm talking about getting some business advice if you don't have any, because most of us don't. I mean let's be honest about it. Most of us grew up with our families working at jobs and society telling us that this is the way life works, and this is what you do. You go out and you get a job, and you work at it; and you go home and you watch TV. And that's it. But the fact is, in business, there's many more dimensions to it. The information on how to become very dynamic and prolific in business is very much sheltered from us. It's exciting to see shows like Donald Trump's *The Apprentice*, where there are amazing amounts of interest and insights – well, the first season anyhow. But I don't know that most people get it. So, you have to be receptive, you have to be open, you have to be looking for it. Of course, it's important to feed your mind all the time and to actually apply the principles in your day-to-day life. So when you get your own business going, the opportunity's now there to apply it, to get things going and to get it started.

HAVE YOUR PATH LAID OUT

What else needs to happen that is totally essential, without a doubt one of the most important things, is to know where it is you want to go. I cannot stress this enough – having goals. Even if you sit down, really quick on a piece of paper, and just write down what it is you want to do. In five years and in one year, and break it down into what you want to do next month. Just scratch it out real quick. Don't think about this. Don't talk about it, because talk is cheap. But actually physically pick up a pen or pencil, and commit it to paper. You will be amazed at the results.

If you hired a very high-priced consultant, the first thing they would likely ask you is this: "Where do you see yourself in five years?" I coach many people in my industry to help them run their photography studios, and the first thing I do is exactly that. I help them get clarity. I don't know the answers for them. But I help them develop their own answers. Because I know that when you develop your own direction, when you know where it is you want to go in five years, you increase your likelihood of success a million times. I cannot stress this enough. So, it's important to write it down. If you stopped reading right here and only took that piece of advice to heart, it would be a million times worth the investment.

What is really good, if you want to get very good at this, is to do this every month on an ongoing basis. Or if you have a goal-setting group in your town or your city that meets every month, a mastermind group of sorts, join them and make goals for each month. Have different kinds of goals. You need a financial goal. You need a lifestyle goal. You need personal goals. You need goals that will help you and your family. You need goals that will help your mind. You need goals that will help your bank account. You need goals that will help your ability to take better photographs, and on and on, and on. Do you know what I mean?

KNOWING WHAT YOU WANT

When you know what you want, you get what you want. I know that goal setting is an old concept that we have all been beat over the head with over and over, and over again. But I'm saying it again, because I believe it. And I've seen it work, too many times, especially when you start with that five-year plan, vision and goal. That five-year picture is probably going to be the hardest picture of all for you to paint. But start it out on a piece of paper.

Write down: 'Five years from now my studio will look like this. I will be making this much money. My health will look like this. My family will be such and such, and such. We'll be doing this, and traveling here and there. And I'll be producing these kinds of pictures, in this field and that field.' And whatever it is you want, let your imagination go wild. And don't get totally retentive about this, in the sense that you stop putting things down, because you think they have to be perfect. Write them down, they're going to happen.

You might think to yourself "what if, what if?" The worst thing to think is "what if?" It's like a poison, worse even. There are no "what ifs"; there are only "can do's." What happens is, we think "what if," and we think, 'Well, if this happens, what if I decide that I don't actually want that?' Hey, nothing says you have to commit to it. You get to be completely flexible when you play this game. Goals can be changed and modified over time, but I cannot stress the importance of writing them on a regular basis.

Trying doesn't work. You know, when you try to do something, it doesn't work because it often involves thinking and half-hearted efforts doing works. Trying doesn't. Some people think that I've achieved a fair amount of success in my business. And I know others who have. But, you know, my answer is this: That after 25 years, I am now an overnight success. That's a quote by my mentor, Dan Kennedy. I've heard him say that, and I thought that is so true. It takes times, but it also takes effort to get things started, to put things into action. So once you make a decision – and that's where your goals will help you out immensely – you get clarity.

Oh, and I should mention too, that once you do that (once you get clarity), opportunities will show up in your life. I can guarantee you, from the bottom of my heart. Chance meetings, the right people, small events, big events, synchronicity – you will notice that things will happen to you. I've seen this happen over and over again, where all of a sudden doors begin to open.

THE FEAR FACTOR

And you know what? You're probably going to get scared. And that's good. Because where there's fear, there's opportunity. Where there's fear, there's a chance for you to grow – not only to grow in business, but also to grow as a person. Because the more you overcome those fears, the better and stronger you become as a person. You become a better person. They actually help mold you into becoming a better person and into becoming more of who you were meant to become. So it's an awesome journey. I suggest that getting off your butt is probably the biggest advice that I can give to anybody. It all starts with your own desire. It also starts with your success as a person, first and foremost. Succeeding as a person before you succeed in business and maintaining a continuous non-stop development of your success as a person, parallels the success of your business. Do not let your fears rule you.

There are more dimensions to the development of yourself. I feel they're important to get into before we get into the actual business of photography, I want to stick with the business of the individual and who you are as a person and the reflection of your business on you. Let's just talk a little bit more about that. In my monthly coaching meetings that I put on in my city, we talk about cleaning up your messes, cleaning up your debts, if you have any addictions, if you have any major issues in your life, that these need to be resolved before you can really move on and develop your business as a whole. It'll prevent you from achieving a lot of goals. The fact is, people have enough messes in their lives to go for a year and a half, to two years, before they really get a handle on them. So don't despair. Don't look at the whole pile of them and say, "Ahhh, I'll never get this done." What you want to do is take one at a time – one a month, and eventually get through the pile.

Sometimes we think messes are messes, but in reality all they are guilty feelings about events from the past. This is a different story. You have to let go of the past in order to get on with the future. If you have anything that you feel bad about, it in no way, shape, or form will reflect who you are now or where you're going in the future. So I urge you to let it go; get over it. Turn any negative feelings from the past, negative experiences; turn them all into a positive. Convert them. Take the energy from those negative experiences and convert them into positive experiences. Use them to help develop your business acumen, your business decision skills, your business abilities and your photography skills, as well. Why not?

BEING TRUE TO YOURSELF – AND YOUR MENTORS

Like I said earlier, your business is a reflection of who you are, and your photography skills are as well. So take every aspect of yourself – good and bad – and develop it in a wholesome way. Besides, if you don't let go of the past and you still feel guilt, it is definitely going to be a mess until you do. It will hold you back. Messes are like six foot thick walls of concrete that are thirty feet high. Imagine you're going down the highway and you see this huge concrete wall; that highway represents your journey. You're heading towards your goals. All of a sudden you've got this huge wall, six feet thick, insurmountable. That wall represents the messes or mess in your life. So we have to clear them out.

It's important to have mentors, as well. In my life, I really latched onto the idea of mentoring when I was about five years into my photography business. One of the guys who influenced me was Steven Rudd out of Toronto. He was a very enthusiastic and a very creative photographer, and also a very successful businessman. His main product was wedding photography. I saw him speak at a seminar, and I saw his work. This was my first seminar. And thank God it was my first seminar, because had I gone to anyone else, I may not have been impacted the way I was. I really got what he was saying and what he was all about; and it totally inspired me. And from that point on, I didn't let go as far as going out there and attending as many seminars and workshops, and buying as many books and videos as I could get my hands on.

A TALE FROM THE ROAD

I have to backtrack a little bit and tell you about what really is my very first seminar, which was a year before I went to this Steve Rudd seminar. I was invited to go to a photographers meeting. I was on their list because it was in my city, and I was a professional photographer. Actually, I had a studio; I advertised in the Yellow Pages and I had an established business of sorts. So, I naturally received correspondence from our Professional Photographers Association. And I mostly ignored them for whatever reason. And finally I decided, well I'm going to check this out; and I went to a meeting.

The door was closed where the meeting was being held at a local hotel. I arrived about 5 or 10 minutes too late. It was a Sunday. I was too shy to open the door and walk into the meeting. I was also hungover. You've got to remember, I was in my early 20's, so I liked to party like a lot of us did back then; probably more so than what was good for me. So I was a little shaken and nervous from that. I was just a very shy person to begin with in many ways. My fears for a good part of my life really affected me and held me back. So that first meeting, I didn't even reach down and grab the doorknob and enter the room.

Does it matter? I don't know. But what's instructive in all of this is that I was held back, and I allowed myself to be held back by my own fears, by my own limitations. A lot of it was naivety and innocence and my own behaviours, and I was very irresponsible back then. Even though I had a full-fledged studio and a part of me was very ambitious and hardworking, I still lacked the ability to go out there at that time, and develop my brain and attend these important workshops. Had I not gotten over that, who knows where I'd be today? I might be on a totally different track, going down the wrong road. I might be a totally different person; and it might be pretty scary. But I didn't. The next year I went to the seminar that I went to and spoke of so far in this book and it was amazing; absolutely amazing. From that point on, it changed my life. I kept an open mind. Since then, I have always kept an open mind to learning and to becoming more educated.

THE IMPORTANCE OF TIME

Let me talk about time for a bit. Your time is very important because what you do with it, will determine where you end up. It's important to use your time, not only in a very constructive and regimented fashion, but to use it so that you can get away from working at work that is the least productive work. For instance . . . and this is okay at first . . . when you're starting your studio, you've got to put in more time doing the grunt work – it's a lot more labour intensive. You've got to put in more hours getting established, getting things done.

Eventually, you want to be able to delegate all this stuff that can be done by somebody for a minimum wage so that you can do the stuff that is important and that you enjoy. The stuff that I'm talking about is the marketing, the stuff that creates sales, not putting together frames or trimming prints or sitting at a computer retouching. You want to get away from that because that's hourly wage work. If you want to really be successful and get to the point where you are producing enough income every year that you can virtually do whatever it is you want to do in your life, then you have to delegate your time and regiment it very, very carefully.

What I did in my life was I looked at my week, and I sectioned off each day to studio activities, to marketing activities. I dedicated Monday night for one thing, and Tuesday, Wednesday, and Thursday for other things. Friday and Saturday were always family; I'd spend time with my wife and my daughter. Then most Sunday nights I would get back at doing marketing and putting together my studio newsletter, or whatever it is I had to do that I couldn't get done during the week because I was busy taking photographs. But I felt it was important that I had to get it done, so I had to work at night.

You see I, never watched TV. TV, in my opinion, is not a very good use of time. All things in moderation are okay, I guess. But I've never really liked watching TV, and I guess that makes me somewhat of a freak. That makes me very much the exception to the rule. I just don't understand it; I don't get it. I don't see what the thrill of watching a weekly series is. I've never even really understood how watching Seinfeld or any of those shows . . . Just don't get it. That's me. So I had a lot of hours during the week open up to me and become available, because of that attitude. I understand that most people are not like that. But it's important, nevertheless, to not over-saturate your life with TV. If you're going to watch TV, and I would recommend you do so in moderation, remember you're working on your dream. You're working on your vision. And if TV is your vision, then you will be stuck in a fantasy land.

CHAPTER 3

What They Won't Teach You in Photography School

*"We are what we repeatedly do.
Excellence, then, is not an act but a habit."*

- Aristole, 384-322 BCE
(Greek philosopher, student of Plato and
teacher of Alexander the Great.)

An education in photography is good. I never want to talk anybody out of getting an education because it can only help in the long run. But what's important to remember is that it is not an essential. It is not a requirement. For photographers, you don't go take a program, follow procedures, get a degree or diploma, and all of sudden you're qualified. It's not that cut and dry. It's not black and white. As a matter of fact, some of the most successful photographers that I know, and I would include myself in there, have very little formal, post-secondary education.

When you look at the statistics, it's probably dismal. The majority of graduates from photography courses probably end up working at retail jobs or in completely different fields. Maybe there's a reason why this happens. I'm not 100 percent sure why that is, but I can only speculate. One thing I do know is that in photography school, as in any school, in any field, there's a lot of stuff that they don't tell you – there's the reality, there's the stuff that you learn when you're out there in the real world fighting the fight, battling the battle of staying in business and working with clients day-to-day, belly-to-belly, nose-to-nose, eyeball-to-eyeball, toe-to-toe, trying to earn a profit so that you can build your business to a prosperous level, and a profitable level, where you will be able to support the lifestyle that you've decided upon.

But I can remember in my struggling days how tough it was. And this is the stuff they never taught, or they don't teach in school. I know of other photographers who have very similar experiences. I'm sure there are many photographers who won't even tell you about them, but they're out there. Maybe there are reasons that they won't tell you about their struggles, the tough road that they took. And it's different for everybody. Some photographers go through this much quicker than others, either through a twist of faith, good fortune, ability on their part to recognize the shorter path to success, or for some like myself, I've decided, and had decided, to take a longer path. But short, medium, or long path, whichever way you take, it's important to note that you will get there if you persist long enough. The journey will take you to a prosperous and successful conclusion for the most part, as long as you follow the right strategies and have a good product, and do the right kind of marketing.

THE DARK SIDE

Some of the darker side includes the moments of despair when, for example, your rent is due, when your payments are due, when there's very little business. You put up with this for several months in a row, or perhaps even several years in a row. It's hard. When I look back at my own history, it's almost like as if it was part of my training. I am personally to blame for the hard times that I went through because I always had a very easygoing attitude. I don't know what it was, call it faith, but I just knew that at the end of the month I would pay the bills. Many other photographers would never be able to work their business that way because their stress threshold is way less.

For me, it was not a problem because I just do not respond to stressful situations like that. However, when you do have rent to pay and other bills, it's a responsibility and a duty to make sure that your business is set up with enough income and that your efforts are going to produce that income so that you can take care of those responsibilities. If it does bother you and stresses you out, it's not going to help the growth of your business.

To the opposite extreme of that example is when people wait until everything's perfect. They wait until everything is ideal. They wait until there's an absolute 100 percent guarantee that they will succeed. Well the fact of the matter is, there are no guarantees. At some point in your life, depending on your comfort zone, you have to leap from one branch to the next and hope that you land on the other branch. You have to, obviously, do as much due diligence, preparation, and planning as is possible. You can take incredible amounts of steps to just try and make sure as much of it sticks, so that you can increase your chances of success.

When I was building my business, I just took massive amounts of steps, a good deal of which was useless. If I had to do it all over, I could easily save heaps of time, perhaps as much as 70 or 80 percent of the amount I invested initially. But I didn't know any better back then. And they didn't teach that in any workshop, and what limited amount of college that I did have.

The real world teaches you something different than the academic world. And in many ways this is where we separate the winners from the losers. This is where we separate those who are bound to succeed to those who are going to end up doing something else, perhaps even taking on real jobs.

I can remember a friend of mine – this is way back when – calling me in absolute despair that things were beyond hopeless, that things were bleak in his photography business. It was a pretty desperate call. And I can remember the sense that I had from this gentleman's situation. He wasn't a happy camper. But I can also recall that I, too, had been there. And I couldn't really offer him much. There was no easy solution to help him pull out of the dilemma that he found himself in. He was struggling. Business wasn't there. And I didn't know any better. What I could say to him now is, "Yeah, I can understand what you're saying 'cause I, too, have been there. But I persisted."

So there's a level of faith that comes into play, assuming you're not being a lazy bum or you have some terrible cloud of messes in your life, assuming that you are working at your business, working as smart as you possibly can, and not plunking yourself down in front of your TV eight hours a day, instead of doing what you need to be doing to get the job done. If you're doing everything that is possible, and you have a certain amount of faith, you'll get there. It's sometimes going to be a slow process, but you'll get there. You have to take it one step at a time. That's how you build the castle – one brick at a time. That's how you build a bridge – one brick at a time.

THE CONCEPT OF INERTIA

There's an idea that hard work is inertia. It creates its own energy. But once you get the ball rolling, the ball rolls. It gets to a point where, if you can imagine, a big giant ball is rolling along at a good, steady pace. All you need to do at that point and time is push it with your index finger to keep the momentum going. But initially getting that ball rolling takes an immense amount of work, takes an immense amount of discipline.

The thing that creates the ability to stick through it is different for everybody, but at its root and fundamental level, it has to do with your desire. It has to do with your level of commitment, your ability to see in your own mind where it is you want to go, what it is you want to achieve, what kind of life it is that you want to create for yourself and your family. That's why, when I coach somebody, the first thing I have them do is create a 5-year plan – where do you see yourself in five years? Of course I can't fill in the blanks for them. They have to do that.

I can urge them along and keep asking the question, "Where do you see yourself in this area? Where do you see yourself in that area? What kind of photography do you see yourself taking? What kind of income do you see yourself producing every year, every month? What kind of clients do you see yourself working with? What kind of a studio do you see yourself working in? What kind of assets do you see yourself owning?" Get a vision of that, and that will help you through the bleak periods. That'll help you through the dark zone, the twilight zone, those moments when all there seems to be is desperation and a lack of faith.

Other influences that urge us forward, and this is something that is rarely talked about, are anger, revenge and jealousy, and some of the other negative emotions. If you've ever read success books like *Think and Grow Rich*, and other books by noted authors such as Napolean Hill, they often talk about the positive emotions and the negative emotions. The negative emotions are the ones that you want to avoid. But the truth of the matter is oftentimes, negative emotions, such as jealousy, revenge and anger, in many ways, push us forward. So, it's important not to dismiss these emotions, but to recognize that, hey, they will sometimes serve a purpose in our success.

Now I'm not talking about being angry or being jealous, and letting those emotions tie us down permanently. What I'm talking about is using them and converting them into a positive direction – this is something that we don't talk about. You can be inspired to succeed because somebody told you you couldn't. Or because somebody told you or did something to you that was a bad turn, and it gave you a real bad feeling. It made you angry. It made you want to succeed even more. And that's okay. The sweetest form of revenge is success. When they say you can't do it, you prove them wrong.

What about jealousy? You don't have to be stuck in the state of jealousy, but you can achieve as much as or more than the other person that you aspire to be like. If you just stay in a state of jealousy, you'll never get anywhere. If you stay in a state of envy, you're limiting yourself forever. But if you recognize that, hey, I would like to have that, too. But don't use that as your only guidepost. If you urge yourself onward, you can help let jealousy and envy help you create your own vision.

There is an inertia to work and action. Once you get that ball rolling, once you list all the steps and all the things, and all the actions that you can take – big, medium, or small – and you just start doing them. Do whatever you can with whatever resources you have instead of saying, "I can't do that because I haven't got this." Don't limit yourself. What you have to do is look at all the things you can do, and work with what you've got. That'll get the ball slowly moving; maybe not as fast as you would like to get it at first, but movement in the right direction is better than no movement.

LOCATION, LOCATION, LOCATION

There's this mindset that you need a good location in order to achieve a successful business. That's a very narrow way of thinking. The fact of the matter is, for photographers, and in a portrait studio, you can pretty much operate your studio anywhere you want, meaning, if you have people to photograph, and if you market yourself properly, they should and will come to you.

Now there are certain influences that will determine whether or not you need to have a certain size studio at a certain location. For example, if you're working with the lower quality, lower price packaging and you want to get a staff and you have a very systematic approach, almost like a franchise, fast food type of scenario, and there's nothing wrong with that type of picture; I know photographers who do quite well running that kind of studio, it's a personal choice.

If you run that kind of a scenario, obviously, you are better suited in a location that is more accessible and a location that is in a busier area of town. Now do you absolutely need to pay for a storefront or expensive mall traffic? You can if you wish, but make sure it pays for itself. But, I don't think you absolutely or necessarily need it. Once you follow certain marketing strategies, and you stay in touch with your clients, they'll come to you. But it is important in that scenario to be somewhat accessible. Don't narrow your thinking on location.

If you were creating a higher end product, a more expensive product, they'll come to you just about anywhere. Obviously you want to avoid certain areas where there might be a risk factor for them going out there, but you have a lot more flexibility. You have a lot more ability to choose locations that are a little more difficult to get at. As a matter of fact, my studio is in an obscure location. And nobody would really know it's there, other than the clients who have called me, contacted me, or come to me on a regular basis.

So, one of the mistakes that is often done, and that you want to avoid, and that they won't teach you in school, is the "location is important" mindset. But it's not really. It's not a black and white situation. High priced, high visibility does not automatically equate success. You have to think about this and make a wise decision. As a matter of fact, I'd like to talk about this from a different angle and it's a point that I bring up over and over again, and that is that men are particularly bad for this. And that is, spending money to try and stimulate business growth by spending money on more toys and such. The default situation or thinking is, we'll buy a solution.

Well, getting a very expensive mall location or a very expensive studio location anywhere, just because it's expensive and you're throwing all kinds of money at it, does not equal success. It's easy to get blinded by this for some people. So I caution you to open up your thinking and not to get stuck in that kind of thinking that is truly distorted. Throwing money at a problem or at a situation in and of itself will not create the solution. As a matter of fact, money in many cases will be a detriment and not a positive thing. When you absolutely have to find the solution with very limited funds, you create much more innovation, much more creativity. You find solutions that are practical and workable much easier without money.

Let me give you another example. I've coached people where they had offices in their homes, and in their mind they thought that that was a very negative thing. They would bring clients into their home, and there would be maybe toys around and you would know it was their home. And they thought that that was a bad thing; that the perception of who they were was going to be seen in a negative light. After I talked about this a bit more, they saw things differently, and hopefully you will, too.

When you have a situation like that, for example, and you are working out of your home, your photography business is at best in a small office adjacent to your family room on the lower level of your home, don't worry about it. Turn what you might perceive as a negative into a positive. If anybody ultimately, and I don't think this would really happen, is annoyed by it, you probably don't want them as a client anyway. The fact of the matter is, you can turn all of that stuff into positive marketing material. You actually should incorporate it into your newsletters, your sales letters, your business cards, your website, because people love relating to other people and their lives. So instead of thinking that your home office, your dinky little home office, with the toys that are strewn about the floor, is a negative thing, have fun with it.

Poke fun at yourself. Tell people how your life is busy because you have these children or that you are "stuck in a small home studio, but wouldn't have it any other way." Someday you may get a big studio, but you're happy in your little home studio with your little office because really what matters is not the location. What matters are the images that you're producing. Your message that you convey from the heart, and the relationship you have with your clients. You can actually use these situations as a springboard to other, bigger marketing messages that you may have.

Do you understand what I'm saying? Simple isn't it? And it works. It works because ultimately, it's all about people relating to people. And people anywhere, it's universal – its universal truth anywhere in the world relates to other people for the most part.

MAKE SURE THE EQUIPMENT WORKS – IN MORE WAYS THAN ONE

Along with choosing the right studio, is choosing the right equipment. And it's really the same message that I talked about. You don't want to throw a lot of money at equipment hoping that having the latest, greatest, most powerful, expensive lens and equipment and all, is going to create solutions for you. As a matter of fact, I would challenge anybody to go buy the oldest, used, beat up camera and just focus on honing their photographic skills with that. Getting a big powerful camera is not going to make you good at analyzing light, creating poses, creating excellent rapport that resonate with people or composing images for ultimately what is very high impact images that resonate with people. You won't get that just by throwing money in the well. I mean it's nice to have really good equipment, but don't get distracted by what really matters and what will truly help you become a better crafts and business person.

A lot of the points I'm talking about here are messages that are true for any business. I mentioned it before that all businesses started at the kitchen table. All businesses started on a shoestring budget with a bunch of notes scratched on a notepad or a napkin. And it all started with great ideas that evolved and were modified and put into practice, and ultimately was of service to the community and to your world.

It's important to focus on what's important, not get distracted by what we might think of ourselves as artists. That we have some divine authority, because we are photographers, we are wizards of light. We think we are in a special category. We're business people – business people first. Being a good businessperson means being a good person, and it will create a better skill set for us. And in turn we will become better photographers.

THE IMPORTANCE OF DELEGATION

Ultimately you want to be able to delegate just about everything that is not essential to creating your business and your marketing. You need to shoot and market, delegate everything else. Simple formula. Unless you are just starting out. In that case you may need to do a lot of the grunt work yourself, but as soon as is humanly possible you need to get rid of everything that is not essential to your business growth. You wouldn't delegate the two most important jobs, unless you're creating a high volume franchise type operation where you're going to have staff doing the pictures because the lights are locked and set and everything is done on a higher volume, lower price basis. But it's still important to understand a lot of the essentials – the posing and good image capture.

So that can be delegated in that scenario.

But as most of us know, we are the photographers. So we essentially don't delegate the photography. The marketing, as well, should never be delegated. All things marketing, and all things strategy, are best if we are in complete charge. And of course you never want to delegate the chequebook. You want to keep a close eye on all accounts, debits, credits, banks, assets, balance sheets, and income statements. Keep a watchful eye at all times, and never delegate the chequebook. But everything else can and should be delegated, if not now, at least in time.

And it's good to be knowledgeable and experienced in areas that we are going to delegate so that we can create a way to train the others. This is true for most things that need to get done, but not all – for example, accounting. I don't have to learn all things accounting in order to delegate the chequebook. But it's good to understand the basics of reading a balance sheet and an income statement, and of course, knowing how to pay our bills on time and how to pay ourselves first. It's good to understand all things about digital workflow. For the kind of work that we're doing, we don't absolutely have to be able to do it ourselves all the time, but it's good to have a good understanding so that we can delegate it. And we know what we're looking for.

All jobs that are best done by somebody at a minimum wage will be best delegated, so that we can do the stuff that is going to pay us maximum return, maximum dollar. Of course at first, when the money isn't there and the business isn't there, we're everything. And that's okay. That's part of the process. But as soon as you start growing, even on a smaller scale, you want to start delegating. And this can be our worst enemy.

All too often, small business people end up being what's called the rugged individualist. They end up doing everything themselves and getting the sense and satisfaction out of that, and somehow linking that to their purpose – their purpose in life and their purpose in business. They end up putting in long hours. After so many years of doing that, and living a life where there's a real lack of balance, they end up with unhappy lives, broken marriages, and broken dreams because they didn't delegate a lot of the stuff that they should have delegated.

But when you start delegating, essentially, what happens is you come into your own being when you delegate all the stuff that you either can't stand doing or should not be doing, because it doesn't give you the highest level of satisfaction. So, don't get caught up in thinking that just because you're trimming prints for seven hours a day and work flowing images for five, and putting images in albums, and doing all that grunt work. Don't fool yourself into thinking that that is high quality work with a deeper sense of purpose. There is stuff that is at a higher level, much more important for you to do. And if you think that taking photographs, creating portraits, isn't there, then you ought to be doing something else.

If you think that marketing and strategic business decision making skills should be delegated (bad move) or it's something you simply can't do that well, then you really should have a good look at your business and your photography studio. Because part of my whole theme in this book is to point out that we are businesses. Understanding this point is essential.

We are running businesses. When you run a business, and you turn a profit, as photographers, not as artists, an odd thing happens. You achieve a much higher level of satisfaction and joy.

Creating businesses and doing all that is necessary in marketing, doing all that is necessary in strategies for business, is actually very exciting, very stimulating. It's a lot of fun. At first, for many of us, it seems like an obscure skill, or it seems like we are compromising the integrity of the art by taking on the business.

This is false thinking. You don't want to do that. I said it before, and I'll say it a million times, that the two are inextricably linked – art and business. Business first, so that you can achieve art. Business first, so that you can become the artist that you were meant to be. And when you delegate everything other than the essential skills that are important to achieving that, then you've become the person, and the artist, and the businessperson that you were meant to be.

The truth is, not too many people will follow this path. And statistically, most of you reading this aren't going to either. I hope you do. I hope you do understand that when you run a business, your photography studio, that as you evolve, things that you delegate increase, and that you start to prioritize the things that are important, and start to delegate the things that are not.

Don't get caught up in that rugged individualist thinking where you are essential to the survival of the business; that if you don't get it done, it's going to fall apart. You don't want to be a perfectionist in this area. When you delegate, good is good enough. And this is an area we often find ourselves getting in trouble. We think that in order to get things done, we have it done our way. You need to lighten up and understand that everybody that you delegate work to is not going to do it exactly the way you want to do it. Otherwise, you're going to pull your hair out, drive yourself crazy, and end up right back in square one where you're doing everything yourself and heading down the wrong road again.

When you delegate, when the results are not up to the exact standards that you wanted, you have to ask yourself, "Is it good enough?" Of course you'll always do it differently. You'll probably do it better, or maybe you just think it's better. But is it good enough? And if it's not, adjust; but don't take it over. And accept the fact that good is good enough. If it's good enough, move on. Move on to the next thing, and keep focus on what you need to do and the stuff that's important to you. And keep delegating the stuff that is minimum wage work.

THE FREEDOM FACTOR

It's a sense of freedom that you achieve when you get to that point. And I've mentioned it before, and I'll say it again, that when you achieve that level, and the more that you achieve in the business sense, the better photographer you become, the bigger service you're doing for the art, the more of an artist you become. Weird, but true.

Are you starting to see the picture here? Are you starting to recognize that in order to become an excellent, top notch photographer, that it's linked directly to things of business so that you can achieve a steady flow of clients that will help you hone your skills, and that you can do and focus on only those things that will help feed and fertilize and help you grow your talent. Delegation is a part of that picture.

Some people worry about competition and whether or not there's enough business in a certain size area. There are certain geographic limitations to certain towns. For example, in a town of 1,000 where there are five studios and you want to do 40 or 50 weddings a year. And babies, and families. You would be limited and you're going to have to look outside of that geographic area to see where you can pull that business from. But if you have people, you have business. People love portraits.

There's lots of business for everybody. If you just walk down any road in any city or town in North America, and you knocked on the door and asked whether or not they've had a portrait done recently, when was the last time they had a portrait done, and if it is something that they find that they would enjoy, you'll probably notice that there's a big void there, and there's a lot of room, a vacuum in the marketplace. There's a lot of work out there for photographers, especially good ones. When you can create a good product and you become a good photographer, it gets to the point where word of mouth will feed you as long as you keep on the right track and don't get distracted.

So, don't let limited thinking control you. I've seen cities of 100,000 support massive amounts of photography studios. And I've seen situations like that where it seemed that the more photographers you had, the more business was actually created. There's almost an energy that is created because in the mindset of the general population, there's a mindset of photographers are a part of our life. Having portraits done and created is a part of our life. So if you go down the limited road where all you see is a limitation and lack of business, you're immediately building a wall, and for no reason whatsoever.

Instead of having that attitude, look at the business that is potentially available to you and go out there and scratch the earth. And it'll grow forth a bounty for you. Where you have people, you have business. People are vain. They love portraits of themselves, even if they might say to you, "I hate having my portrait done." Memories of them and their family are essential. They're important to them.

Back in the old days when photography was in its infancy, photographers used to travel from town to town. When they would pull into a town, there would be line-ups a mile long to have a portrait done. Photography had not yet taken on the level that it is at nowadays. It was very much a novelty. But it still spoke to the same human condition that we are all a part of, and that is the preservation of our life and our legacy. So, there is a lot of business out there. Don't be limited.

All you need to do is just show up and there's a ready market for you where you have people. There's always a vacuum. The more people you have, the bigger the vacuum. In our own minds, if we say there isn't a vacuum, fine that's it. That will be your truth that you'll abide by. But if you say to yourself, "Nope, there's a market here; people are people, and they will buy my portraits. And it will stimulate the general population into thinking that way and creating a mindset." Then that's what you will achieve, if that's what you decide to achieve.

LEARN FROM CONFUCIUS

People are very selfish and very vain. We're really always concerned about what's best for us. There's a famous saying by Confucius that a man is more concerned about the boil on his neck than the drowning of a thousand in the Yangtze River. And essentially what Confucius was saying is exactly what I'm trying to tell you, and that is that people are very self-centered. But this is a good thing. Because we're self-centered and vain, and we want what's best for us, portraits are a perfect fit. So whether we're having portraits done of family, portraits done of our children and babies, or the events in our lives, such as weddings and anniversaries, even business portraits, it all fits in there.

It's all part of the same situation – that vanity is the reason why the business is there. And the vanity creates a vacuum for us to fulfill that need, that economic need, that we can build a lifelong business from. Interesting perspective, isn't it? But it's something that I earnestly believe in. And when you get an understanding of basic human concepts and conditions, you understand that no matter where you go, you can create a business. You can create a photography business. When you understand what drives people at a deeper economic level, it gives you more insight, more ability to create more solutions.

There is a lot of business out there. People will spend a lot of money on themselves, on their families. People will spend an incredible amount of money on their children, on the events in their lives. What you have to ask yourself is, "Do you have the product and the ability to move that product from yourself through to their lives so that you can trade that for money?" That's what business is all about. It takes a certain amount of faith, and it takes a certain amount of confidence. It takes a certain amount of strength and confidence to say and make a stand that 'this is what I am, this is what I stand for, and this is what my product is all about. Are you interested?'

And you have to be able to do this without flinching. You have to be able to quote your price and not let them see you sweat. You have to be able to do so, keeping in mind where it is you are trying to go so that you can keep moving forward. Otherwise, you're going to get stuck. You do not want to get stuck in limiting thoughts, limiting mindsets and illusions. So this is the stuff they will not teach you in school. It helps in our field as photographers, because if you look at the very nature of what most photographers are like, I feel very lucky to be a part of this.

Most photographers, it seems to me anyway, in my observations, seem to be very youthful. They seem to be very optimistic and upbeat. Maybe it's the nature of the beast. The fact that we're producing something that is so much fun, and it is such a fun way to earn a living that keeps us useful and optimistic. Whatever the reasons are, it's an observation that I have made.

CHAPTER 4

How to Create a Style That is Uniquely Yours

"In my mind's eye, I visualize how a particular . . . sight and feeling will appear on a print. If it excites me, there is a good chance it will make a good photograph. It is an intuitive sense, an ability that comes from a lot of practice."

- Ansel Adams, 1902-1984
(Photographer/Author/Conservationist)

Creating a photographic style is not something that is easily defined. There are several issues that need to be addressed first. I get asked a lot of questions, especially regarding marketing, from other photographers. A lot of newer, starting-out photographers will ask me marketing related questions; and the first thing I look at is their actual work. And if the work is not there, in all honesty, it's not a good idea to go forward with their marketing quest because you have to look at the work itself.

You have to start with a pretty decent product. That doesn't mean you have to be better than everybody else; you don't have to be top of your field right away. Eventually, if that is your goal, that is okay. But if you decide to even stay average, you can still get into some pretty good marketing and market with a higher volume concept in mind. There's no right or wrong here. All of this works. What's important is to decide for yourself where is it that you want to take this passion that you call photography – to what level would you like to eventually take it? And have a good, solid, honest look at where it is you are at right now versus where it is you would like to go.

HAVE CAMERA, WANT SUCCESS

Now, if your work is not where you would like it to be, there are several things you can do. There's nothing hands down, nothing, absolutely nothing on this planet that will beat experience. You can combine experience with the idea that you're going to use your imagination and push yourself, push the envelope, go beyond your limitations to try and create a style that is uniquely yours. And of course a lot of styles are built on solid fundamental concepts that really will never change.

That's why you see so many workshops, seminars, and so many leaders that teach in photography because they often go back to the fundamentals – fundamentals of lighting, fundamentals of composition, and in all honesty, fundamentals of marketing apply equally as well – as ideals that will never change. They are immune to time and to generations. But you can build on those and create your own style. But you have to be able to master technique. This is so critical that you master technique, and that you know your equipment inside out. This will only come with time and experience. You can only master technique by putting a lot of miles on your camera.

Now, is there a rule of thumb? Is there a hard and fast black and white rule? Absolutely not. It's different for everybody. As a matter of fact, I've been at this game 27 years, and I still feel like I'm just out of the gate and still learning. And I see people, who have started out, and they're only in the game for a couple of years, and they look like they have total mastery over their game, which in and of itself has its own perils. If you start out and you have a God given talent, and through other circumstances you automatically gain some success because a lot of stuff happens to be working in your favour. If you're not aware of that, you may let it go to your head, and your ego might become cemented. And if in time, if you do not evolve or if circumstances need you to evolve and you can't, you're going to be in a real situation that will create nothing but hardship and frustration, eventually.

DEFINING YOUR STYLE

By creating your own style, aside from the fact that you need to really build on your experience, there are other techniques that you can use in order to really define that style. So let's start with the first step, and that is getting experience. You have to get experience now, and it's an absolute must. It is, without a doubt, one of the easiest things to do.

Just like a musician who practices for the symphony, or anybody in any craft, this craft that we call photography requires that you master your tools and that you master light and composition in as many situations as is possible. So you have to get out there and shoot, damn it. Just do it! Get out there and shoot on an ongoing basis.

I don't care if you're going to the circus, on a vacation, you're going to the mall with your spouse, or if you're going for a walk, bring your camera with you and practice all the time. Become obsessed. Light a fire under your butt and get going. Look at images in magazines and/or look at images from other photographers. Try and duplicate. Don't just think about it, do this. Actually get out there and do it.

PRACTICE BRINGS PERFECTION – OR CLOSE TO IT!

You have to practice. Even if you're an old, calcified, experienced crud like myself, it's a really good idea to constantly be pushing yourself, so that way you can remain diversified, resilient and prolific as a photographer who has complete mastery over all elements of his or her craft. So this is important; just as important as it is for a concert playing musician who has to learn and master certain songs by the time the concert happens. They don't show up at the last minute to open up their music and then start playing. Too many photographers do this, and they think they can get a handle on it. Treat it with equal respect and equal attention and due diligence as you would a concert going musician. So get out there and practice as much as you can.

Take on as many jobs as you possibly can when you're first starting out. Do sports teams. Do as many freebies as you can, but don't build a reputation as somebody who does work free all the time. Make it very clear that you're still learning, you're still growing, and you're only going to do this in a temporary situation. So it's important to really, first off, go for the experience.

I did in my profession. I practically took everything I could. There's the story of Ansel Adams who used to photograph schools and school children, and who also was quoted as saying, "I've learned more from the bread and butter aspect of photography than from anything else." And without a doubt, those experiences helped build upon his mastery of his craft, of his game. And you know where Ansel Adams ended up – as one of the world's best photographers of all time. So it's important to, first of all, learn the technique and master the technique. And then it's important to get out there and experience as many different situations as is possible and build on those foundations.

MANAGING YOUR EMOTIONS

And of course, there's the emotional aspect of all this, too. When you're photographing a large group, an individual, small group, a child, a pet, whatever, there are emotional reactions that you will go through as a photographer, as a human being. There are emotional reactions that your subjects will go through. You have to have all of these things under control, or at least you have to be able to manage them. You have to be able to manage them and take them so that they work with you and help maximize your end product – a great portrait.

If you are in a situation where you're photographing people and you do not manage your emotional reaction, the people, your subjects, may get very nervous, and it will potentially backfire or spin out of control. You have to be able to work from point 'A' to point 'B' and manage all aspects, including your emotions, and as best you can, your subjects, and get the job done. If you're not used to this, if you don't master this to a degree, and you fall apart, your work's going to suffer.

That's another reason why you should be practicing all the time, especially practicing the type of photography that you want to be doing. Of course we're talking mostly about pictures of people. And I qualify pictures of pets as well, because there are very similar approaches that are required when photographing pets, just as you would photograph human beings. To develop your style, start there. And that's just the beginning. Really, it's just the beginning. You have to build upon that.

The beautiful thing about all of this is that once you do manage to get a handle on it, you essentially have it for life. You never forget. And you're able to build on and progress beyond that. So you have to keep an open mind and remain resilient so that as you build upon it over the years, and even over decades, you become a master of the craft.

One issue that often happens to a lot of photographers is that they get very impatient. They assume it's a black and white, very procedural situation. Well, it's more than just a procedure. It's more than just do this, do that, get the job done. It, again, takes years of experience so that you can manage to master technique, and then master creativity. Do this, be patient, take your time, build upon it, and keep the big picture in mind, and you are guaranteed to succeed in time.

This is an area where we often separate the serious players from those who are not so serious. This is the area where we can really determine who is going to have staying power, who's going to last, who's going to develop their own style, and who's going to develop a great product with which to take part in? So, that's what it's all about – creating your own style.

THE IMPORTANCE OF SWIPE FILES

Another great technique to help you along is swipe files. I love using swipe files. I have photographs that I've clipped out of magazines. I had my daughter cut them out neatly and tape them onto pieces of paper that are now in a binder. Those are for weddings. I have that binder in my car, so when I'm heading out to a wedding, I sometimes will stop for coffee and peruse this binder full of ideas. I'll make notes in there. I'll put in some of my own photographs just to remind me to do certain poses. I'll borrow these ideas, because ideas can never be copyrighted.

Ideas are there for us to use. So we might as well use them. What you want to do is grow these ideas and innovate them as best you can. If you make a blank copy of a pose, that's okay, too. That's perfectly acceptable. Sometimes you're thrown into a situation with a pre-planned mindset, a certain pose that you know you are going to create, and through whatever circumstances and/or situations that may be thrown at you, you'll develop an impulse, an idea, a creative thought with which to take that idea and bring it up to a whole new level. Run with those impulses. That's what it's all about. You can't do that if you're still struggling with technique. You can't do that if you're still struggling and trying to manage emotions. Managing these areas are essentially the first stepping-stones to creative nirvana.

Another great way to use swipe files is through websites. I have a folder on my favourites folder that I call 'Inspiration'. It's really just a list of bookmarks from other photographers that I've visited over the years. Photographers whose work I find inspiring. Whenever I feel like just being inspired, I'll go online, go to that folder, and start going through that list and looking at some of the poses that have affected me. Poses I thought were really great and that I would like to duplicate. I'll look at some of the poses that maybe are new, because a lot of photographers will update their websites with new ideas. It's just a great way to have easy and fast access to instant swipe files using the inspiration and ideas from other photographers.

Another great idea for swipe files is movies. I love going to movies, and I love renting movies. It's one of my favourite activities. And I'll notice – and I get better at this and so will you – composition. I notice lighting. I even notice posing. Just look at the theme where an actor or an actress will be playing a huggie, romantic, kissy type scene filled with emotion. And you'll catch little micro-glimpses. You can slice time up and notice the way certain events can be frozen into little images forever, memorialized. I notice that all the time – composition and lighting. Notice the way they use lighting in certain movies, and you'll get a lot of ideas.

You'll get a lot of inspiration from these images that you'd like to create on your own. What's great about this is if you borrow ideas from the mass media, especially if they can somehow either subconsciously or consciously be directly linked to a very popular movie, people will relate to and resonate with them. These ideas are fresh, they're new, and they're what people generally are used to and see all the time. Use them to your benefit.

You can get a lot of great ideas from music videos, as well. People instantly make a connection there. They don't know why, they just make a connection. The reason is because pop culture is so much a part of their lives, and you're borrowing some of these ideas from pop culture and you're incorporating them into your photography. It's important in many ways to pay attention when you're watching movies and when you're renting movies, or when you go to the cinema, or if you're watching the music channel.

Look for new ideas and new inspiration at all times. They're there. They're pervasive. We are saturated with all kinds of creativity in our society, and it's called pop culture. Use it as best you can. And when you do, you're automatically speaking the language with which today's culture resonates and is familiar with.

As I mentioned before, I'd like to include magazines in there as well, because magazines are loaded with ideas – bridal magazines, fashion magazines, men's health magazines, you name it. Just about any magazine that is specific to a certain gender, age, and/or sex, will be loaded with ideas that are fresh, that are new. If you read some of the articles, too, or even capture some of the headlines, you might get some of the issues that are sensitive to today's group of people that you're marketing to. That way you can become more sensitive to what it is that may be important to them either through photography or even through marketing. If you become more aware of what it is that's important to them, you can really tap into that through magazines and different media. You should be able to address those concerns, and you'll get some ideas that are photographic in nature or marketing in nature. Who knows?

THE ZEN MASTER

One thing that happens when you do develop a style, when you develop a mastery over technique, if you remain prolific and resilient, and you remain open – it's very important to remain open – if your mastery almost becomes so second nature that it looks extremely easy to the outside viewer, when your mastery looks almost like it's effortless. This is a good thing. This is pretty much where you want to go. I call this a Zen-like confidence. It's a free flow river of ideas and creativity that just pours out of you, and into your work, and into the heart and soul and mind of your clients. It affects you on all levels.

It affects you in the way you interact with your clients, from first meeting to actual session, to the sales process, to the actual photography sessions. Your sense of style and confidence that you develop when you create your style affects you on all levels. It's a good by-product and a good thing to go after when you're developing your own style.

It's easy to get distracted here, you know? You want to be very careful. Be forewarned not to get distracted by too many obsessions over equipment, software, or other technical issues. You really want to use your imagination. Einstein was credited with saying that 'the most important thing in life is imagination'. What he would do is look at all the basic facts about a certain area and then totally let go of them, totally ignore them, so that he could go into a free flow thinking process with which he could then develop new ideas.

But, of course, a guy like Einstein, he had a pretty good technical idea, first off. And that's why you need that, too, so that you can get into that free flow state. But it's easy to get caught up into left-brain thinking where, 'Well, you know, if only I can get this piece of equipment,' or 'I absolutely must have that lens,' or 'If I get that software then I too will become a better photographer'. So we make that association. But the truth of the matter is, it's much more to it than that. It's all the things that I've been talking about so far, underscored by the idea that we need to put it into action. Pull the cork and let go.

I recently attended a workshop put on by a photographer whom I feel is an excellent photographer, and who developed a creative style with certain use of light and lighting that I thought was completely innovative. I wanted to learn this. It was a struggle for me to learn it because there were some technical issues with the light that required me to read the manual (ugh!), learn how to set up the lights, and then to put it into practice. But I got there.

I quizzed this speaker and went back to quiz him some more because I kept struggling, but eventually I did get it. Then I had to put it in practice, because as I soon discovered, and I'm sure you will discover as well, when you're learning something new, once you get out there in the field and you put it into practice, it's not that easy. You see this speaker that I'm speaking of and using as an example had years and years, and years of mastery over this technique. I'm sure he struggled at first. One thing the speaker told me is that whenever he goes into a situation, he said to me, "I always try and challenge myself to come up with something new."

I thought that was pretty cool. I thought that was a great way to look at things. But it's often going to be more challenging, more difficult, and more of a struggle if you don't have that sense of control or that mastery over your equipment and the technical side, or if you get distracted by other issues that are not important. So, once I did this and managed to get a sense of mastery over the equipment, I still didn't have it because I had to get out there and now apply it in the field. And I experienced nothing but frustration and lousy results. But did I give up? Absolutely not.

The idea here is not to give up. You have to keep pushing yourself so that you get those little breakthrough moments, those little revelations, those little sparks of light and awareness in your mind, where you go, "Ahah! There it is." And now you take that and you run with it to a whole new level; and then from there, your own style develops.

YOUR PASSION WILL PUSH YOU THROUGH

You have to be able to work with situations and push your way through. It takes passion, you know. It's good that you have passion for your craft because that will be the fuel that pushes you forward. It's good to have the big picture that you want to achieve. It takes guts, and it takes determination to consistently and persistently work through these issues that I'm talking about. And, of course, it takes time and a positive attitude.

I hate to say it, you know it sounds a little bit cliché, but if you have big picture optimism, you can be negative as far as the small details are concerned, and that's okay. But when you're developing a style and you're working through experience and you're working in different situations, it's good to think, "Okay, what's the worst thing that could happen here?", and to be prepared. It's good to have that small detail pessimism, but to remain big picture optimistic. So that way when you get into a situation and things don't work out the way you would like them to, you can say, "I'm going to keep going until I get this, until I get the photographs that I want to achieve and I get the results that I'm looking for". And, if you don't know what that is, well, you just keep going after it, and it eventually will become clearer in your mind.

When circumstances are thrown at you, to remain resilient is to remain flexible, and to remain confident. You know a lot of creativity is nothing more than confidence. Creativity is knowing in your heart and soul and mind, that you will achieve something. If you go into a situation and you think you must get 'X-Y-Z' and the circumstances will not allow you to achieve 'X-Y-Z' and you experience nothing but frustration and depression and anger, you're going the wrong way. You have to remain resilient. Say, "Okay, what else can I achieve? What can I pull out of this?" And that is where you will develop new ideas. Your style will come through, and it's all underscored by your confidence, and your level of determination.

TAKING A CUE FROM MUSICIANS

I often like to talk about musicians when I compare what we need to go through to achieve total creativity, and to develop our own style and success in photography. I think there's a lot of validity in that comparison. A lot of photographers and what they achieve, directly parallels the same process of what a lot of musicians do. With musicians, when they get up on stage and they start playing, if they didn't practice, it's going to be very, very obvious to the whole crowd, because it's such a performance-based art form.

In photography, no one else has to see that photograph unless we decide to show it off. If we're showing off our photographs and it's not quite there, it'll be obvious to our prospects, friends, and/or clients, that what we're producing is pretty crappy. We may fool ourselves into thinking that it's okay and we may be falling in love with our own work, but I caution you to be very brave in this area. One area that you can develop your own style and become much better in is to be able to take constructive criticism. That's why entering print competitions is so difficult for so many people because it's often at first very painful. We anticipate positive results, but we end up with what we think is rejection, and we take it very personal. It's very important to be able to say, "Well I'm going to take this experience and I'm going to use it in a very, very positive way."

I like using the same hard work and determination that many of my favourite bands have gone through over the years as a comparison to success. It all comes together in their performance and style and mastery thereof. I've read about many bands, because I love music, music moves me. Ever since I was a young teenager, I was fascinated by a lot of these bands. As I read up on them I discovered that they had a lot of things in common.

A lot of them started off technically weak. They were not great "musicians", oddly enough. But they were very performance driven. This told me something. This told me that the hard work and the fact that they wanted to play so much that they took every single opportunity to do just that, and that they put their egos aside; if they had any differences, they put those aside, and they did it for one purpose, and one purpose only – their audience.

You can almost always tell a musician and/or a band that plays for themselves and their own egos. They often end up talking too much on stage, talking about things that are completely irrelevant to the audience. They end up going into stories that no one has any idea of what they're talking about. I think that is really, ultimately a marketing issue, but it's also indicative of the fact that a lot of these musicians just aren't getting it. It's not surprising that those are the musicians that are still struggling.

The very successful musicians – take the band U2 for example – they are a prime example. It's common knowledge that they were not very good musicians, but they were so driven to perform on stage and they had such a passion, that that passion came through in their music, and they played for the audience. Here's a band that played, literally at this point and time, over a thousand concerts. If you look at almost all these successful bands, that's the way their experience, their stories evolved.

They played constantly, constantly, constantly. They got very, very good through the act of performing, and that's what music is all about – an act of performing. So we can learn as photographers from that experience and develop our own style in the ways that are unique to photography, but keeping in mind that we have to work hard, and we have to be determined, and we have to gain that experience the same way that these guys do.

A few more examples of bands that I admire for their success and their perseverance are bands like KISS or Lynyrd Skynyrd. These are bands that started out in the '70s and became famous, to a certain degree. And bands like KISS are still very popular. Like them or not, we can all learn from their success. You may not like their music, but that's not the point. What is important and what is instructive for us as photographers, is to look at the process with which bands like this have gone through in order to succeed and develop their own unique style of music.

When KISS started out, as all of these other bands, they all worked extremely hard. They would go to a gig, set up their stage, and those costumes that they wore at the time, they'd put their makeup on and get on stage and play their hearts out. At the end of the gig, they had to strip the makeup off, load up and get back in their vehicle. Oftentimes they did this in the dead of winter. They'd have to go drive another six, seven, eight, or nine hours to go to their next gig, set up again, do it all over, get into their outfits which were still wet with sweat from the concert the night before. This is when they were nobody. This is when they were just starting out. But they did this over and over, and over.

Lynyrd Skynyrd . . . same thing. They played their hearts out. Their music is rather simple, but their music is filled with passion and a unique style that can only be defined by them. That's what we have to do. We have to define a style that is uniquely ours. That's how you get there – by standing up, playing the concert, playing your heart out, giving it all you got, breaking down at the end of the gig, and doing it all over the next day, over and over, and over again.

A CRITICAL MISTAKE

A common rookie mistake is when a photographer picks a great image, then they'll rest on that image as if they have achieved nirvana – 'I've created this image'. They just keep bringing it up over and over again. That's not a good thing because if you rest on your laurels, they'll tend to become wreaths. You do not want to take your success and try and pin them on your chest as if they're going to glow forever and ever.

The fact is that once you create great images, you will get to a point where you're able to do that over and over, and over again. So, it's not just one image or a couple of images that you produce in a short period of time. It's a series of great images that you produce over and over, and over again, as long as you do what needs to be done to get to that point where you're able to do that and then maintain that, consistently in a lifetime. Once you get to that point, maintaining it is not a problem.

It's really quite simple. It's like creating momentum. Let's say you wanted to get this . . . let's compare it to a big, giant 10-foot tall steel ball. It's going to be very, very difficult to get that ball moving. You're going to put your shoulders into it; use your entire body, every ounce of effort you can to get it going. But once you get it going, it's really just a matter of keeping your finger on the ball and rolling with that. If you ever take your finger off the ball, if you ever become lazy or complacent, or if you ever think that you've made it and you don't have to work any more, that's when things will start to disintegrate for you.

THE POINT AND SHOOT

There's another technique that you can use to create your own style, and that is the point and shoot camera. I'm a firm believer that the point and shoot is an amazing learning tool that helps you develop your skill. Why? They're small, they're light, and they're very, very powerful, especially in today's day and age. I bring my point and shoot camera with me everywhere. As a matter of fact, I've achieved some of my best images with my point and shoot camera.

Do I bring that camera with me on regular jobs to get the job done for regular clients? Of course not. But I will bring it with me in case I want to take some video or some photographs with my point and shoot, so that I can have the benefits that a point and shoot camera allow me. Those benefits are easy access to a camera, easy access to the experience the situation will give me so that I can pull my camera out and practice composition, practice lighting, and all the other things that go along with obtaining experience with photography. So it's still a camera and all the rules still apply. Like I said, I've gotten some of my best images that I used as actual award-winning photographs taken with my point and shoot camera – the quality is quite good.

But the idea that you can bring this camera with you anywhere is a powerful idea. Don't put it in the cupboard somewhere. Pull it out and have it with you all the time – day in, day out – so that you're constantly learning and constantly photographing and honing your skills. A point and shoot camera will give you that opportunity.

SEARCHING FOR A SHORTCUT?

Is there a shortcut to all of this? Well, not really. You have to go through the process. And the process is different for each and every one of us. The same fundamental rules apply. You have to get your abilities to a certain level. How long it takes you to get there, it's up to you and your abilities, your determination, your innate parlance. Then again, this is different for everybody; but there are no shortcuts to getting there.

You have to have faith, you have to have the idea of a big picture in your mind, you have to be persistent, and you have to not think about it. You have to put things into action and do. Doing is far more important than thinking. To try is to die, as they say. Don't try – do. Get out there and do it.

Even if you fail, failures are your best lessons. Failures will have more nuggets of truth and potential success than anything else. So when you fail, you have to have the attitude that 'I'm going to look at this failure and look for the opportunities, look for the lessons learned, look for the new direction that I can take because of that failure and avoid repeating it or look at what new direction you can go into'. So if you're failing, you're actually on the right path. Fail fast, stumble along. So if you fail and fall, pick yourself back up, brush yourself off, and keep going. That's the secret strategy. But getting up off your butt and doing it has to happen first.

THE IMPORTANCE OF PEOPLE SKILLS

I should mention, too, that honing your people skills is important. I touched on this somewhat throughout this chapter, but I'd like to mention it again in closing because I think it is far too important. We are portrait photographers, which means we photograph people. And if we can make ourselves better people, better salespeople, better speakers, better communicators, and if we can become better in any way, shape, or form, our work will be better and we will affect the way our unique style evolves, as well.

Do whatever you need to do to become a better person. What is that? What is it you need to do to feel more gratitude in your life? What is it you need to do to achieve better confidence? Most of us know the answers, but we're too afraid. You see, fear is a big, big stumbling block for most of us. It's human nature. It's the flight or fight response mechanism that is inherent in all humans and many, many animals.

When you feel fear, look at that fear and ask yourself, "Where is the opportunity for growth here?" For me, it was public speaking. I was petrified for many, many years as a public speaker. I couldn't do it. In grade school, high school, and what little college I had, fear held me back probably more than anything else. It also kept my social skills, business skills and selling skills locked away until I unleashed them.

Throughout most of my 20's I was incapacitated by this fear. And I didn't really break out of it until I stopped any negative and/or destructive behaviour that only fed that fear. I really took action to try and develop new skills. I learned how to speak in front of groups. I took every single opportunity I could in my life to speak in front of groups. And for a couple of years, it was hard; it was very, very hard. It was very difficult for me. But I persisted.

I am very glad I did, because now I have the skill that I would have never been able to develop, unless I faced my fears dead-on and wrestled them to the ground and almost removed them for at least now they are able to be managed. Now when I speak in front of a group, it's a real sense of mastery for me. That took a total of 13 years to develop. The first two years were very difficult. Was it worth it? The better question to ask is: What price are you really paying when you don't tap into the talents and skills locked inside you by your fears.

You can't let your fears whip you around for the rest of your life. When you manage to get a handle on your fears, look for the opportunity to become a better person and you will become a better photographer. That is a total given. You cannot avoid it. The two are linked. Look at the fears in your life, and see where the opportunity is. When you do this, you not only become a better photographer, you not only develop your own unique style, but it actually helps, for obvious reasons, every area in your life – it will help your business, your marketing skills; it will help your family, your home life; it will open up new opportunities for you, as well.

I'm a big believer in this concept. I have a speech that I've given many, many times, which I started and created when I was asked to do a speech, a one hour speech, to a group of graduating high school students many years ago. I developed this speech called 'Rob's Top Ten Rules for Success in Business and in Life'. And rule number three is, do what you fear. Because when you do what you fear, the opportunities will present themselves for further growth.

Jeff Foxworthy talks about when he was struggling and growing. Seinfeld gave some advice to Foxworthy's big question back then: "How can I create a 'style'?" Seinfeld told him to keep giving his show, keep making people laugh, keep doing it, day after day, month after month, and your style will develop. And it did. Jeff is now a household name.

CHAPTER 5

Sure-Fire Selling Techniques
(or, Shy Photographer-Salespeople Have Lousy Lenses)

"You're only as rich as your employer lets you be."

- James Hodgins
(Photographer of the Year 2002, 2004, and 2005
PPO North Eastern Branch)

D id you know that studies have been done that reveal an interesting bit about human behaviour? When people ask for something from other people, strangers even, and they give them the reason why they want that something, the people being asked are about a hundred times more likely to comply than if they don't give a reason. In other words, if you ask for a favour and you say why you need that favour, your chances of achieving that positive response from the person you're asking increases a hundred times. They don't know why that is, but it's true.

Did you also know that people will not sue their doctors when their doctors have done wrong, if they respect their doctor. If their doctor has been a caring, listening type of individual, as opposed to a doctor who has been cold and unaffectionate. These are some interesting truths about people and human beings, and the way we are. It is good to know when you are learning the art of selling. In a nutshell, tell them why they should buy what you are selling, and be sincere, present and caring. You will touch people at a deeper level. Add to this the fact that you know as much as you need to know about their needs, so you can answer to those specific needs, and you have a winning combination.

It's obvious; when you're going to ask for a sale, give them a reason why. You'll improve your odds dramatically. When you're going to create an ad, put reasons why they should respond. It's such a basic concept. But if you look at most ads, it's not there. Why? Because most people don't know this. Most people agree that even advertising agencies don't understand this. It's a basic fact that we could all use to maximize our selling ability. And when we're creating ads, we're still selling, just as much as if we're selling while we're showing our photographs and trying to sell a certain package.

When we're putting ads together, be it direct mail, magazines, newspaper ads, whatever, even our website, these are all mediums for selling. But once you learn the art of selling, you apply it just as easily to all of these different media. Once you understand human nature, and you make it a habit of studying human nature, you increase your ability to sell. This is just as important as taking on the marketing. And it's just as important as developing your own photographic style and delivering a good product, because without the ability to sell, nothing really gets moved or the phone doesn't ring. Selling is of prime importance. So I urge you to take the ability to sell as a serious, serious issue.

WHEN YOU SEE SELLING AS NEGATIVE

It's an enigma for many of us because selling is often viewed as a real negative thing, or we have, for whatever reason, these culturally influenced views as to what selling really is. And all we can think of is pushy sales people or late-night infomercials. And we make that connection instantly, and we think that all selling is of that nature. But really it's not. There are certain strategies that apply equally to all the effective forms of selling. But in running our photography studios, learning to sell starts at the very basic level of developing a relationship with your prospect. If people like you, they are much more inclined to buy from you. So, that's the first step – be likeable.

If you have a process that makes sense, and you give people reasons why this is important or that is important, and all the different steps that you put them through in your photographic sessions, or if they're responding to an ad, you give them reasons, they will respond in much greater numbers. So you have to apply this ability at all levels and all areas of your marketing and in your photography. Even when you're doing an actual photo shoot, you should be selling. There are ways to do this that make sense and that are non-intrusive, that won't put you in a bad light or won't make the clients feel that you are adding undue pressure on them. So, selling, again, all starts with the individual – becoming somebody that is likeable.

And then it is serving. Really, you're just serving. You're offering options and information, and explaining it in a consultative and constructive way all the different aspects of what it is you're all about. Ignore this at your own peril. Make the assumption that when you're selling, you do have an eager audience. If you're trying to push your message upon somebody who is not in the least bit interested in what it is you have to offer, then basically you're not selling. You're in a situation that you shouldn't be in. It's really stupid. Get out of there.

So selling is not about trying to convince people who are not interested to become interested. Really, selling is all about finding those who have a spark of interest, feeding that interest, fueling and fanning the flames of that fire of interest, so that you can bring it to completion, and hopefully have a long-term relationship with your client.

So selling starts with that in mind, that you are in front of a group of people who are most likely to purchase what it is you have. And, of course, when you are selling the final product – which is the actual photography – and you're selling in the final stages, the actual packages or reprints sell, they are obviously inclined to buy from you at that point and time. And there are different strategies that are going to become important at that point and time. But we'll get to that later.

FIRST THINGS FIRST

First off, let's look at the very initial steps of selling – your first impression. It is so true, our body language says so much about us, and who we are, that we cannot prevent it other than trying to improve upon it. People in the first 45 seconds of meeting you will make several, instant judgments about you. They will instantly judge you upon things like this: How much does this person make? How old are they? And the other question is of prime importance: Should I respect this person?

This happens at a very, very deep and at a very profound subconscious level. So if you have issues in your life, if you have big messes in your life, if you have personality disorders that you feel are in the way, you have to try and improve upon yourself so that when you make the first impression, it comes across in a very positive way.

When people are sold on you, you're in the right direction, right then and there. Instantly.

There are some photographers who are not the most personable people in the world or who may even come across as arrogant. But situations will allow them to sell regardless, because a lot of other things are working in their favour – mainly, their work is outstanding, and also things like they really don't have any other options to find people or photographers at that level in their immediate area or that is easily accessible. But is that a situation that anyone would want? I certainly wouldn't.

I want to improve my odds of maintaining a long-term, successful, repeat clientele scenario with my prospects and clients. So I want to be likeable right away. I want to do my very best to become a very likeable person. That's why when you call my studio, the first thing we say is, "Thank you". We express gratitude. When you call my studio we say, "Thank you for calling Westmount Photography. Rob speaking, or Tina speaking, or Megan speaking."

Whoever's answering the phone says their name. That way you apply a name to that personality, to that initial introduction. And you make yourself more likeable, more real, and more personable by doing so. Is that the only strategy you should be using? Of course not. There's far more to it than that. That's just one very, very small microscopic way in which you can start becoming a better salesperson – is on the phone. That first impression counts, even on the phone.

But when you're live and in person, it has far more impact. Make yourself personable and presentable. Make yourself a person who knows how to exude a personable energy, somebody who telegraphs warmth and magnetism so that when others meet you, they pick up on that right away. These are the essential first steps in selling.

You really do this by getting out of yourself and listening to other people. When you listen well to other people and communicate with them, people will resonate. I'm not saying I have this down pat. I struggle with this all the time, but I know that the more I listen and the more I practice listening, the more I improve my odds of selling. And I ask a lot of questions.

I don't ask a lot of necessarily open-ended questions or questions that'll put people on the defensive. You want to avoid questions like, "Well, why did you do that?" It's important to ask questions that are totally and directly linked to what it is they're trying to achieve. So, for example, if a bride or groom is coming to me and they're considering hiring me as their wedding photographer, I'll ask them about their wedding plans. I'll ask them where they met. These are direct questions with direct answers. And it opens up the conversation.

And as they discuss these answers with me, I will sometimes pick up subtle clues, which will lead me to another question. And so, for example, another question might be, "Oh, so that's important to you. Is it?" They may bring up something to do with something, I'm not sure what, but the question that I can fade away into is just that . . . "That is important to you, is it?" And most of the time, if I ask that type of question, I'll be dead-on; and they'll say, "Yeah, it is important."

And that way I'll get, not only more information with which to take this conversation [sales process] to completion, but it'll also help me create a better product in the long run. They will like the fact that I'm connecting with what it is that is important to them, and in their eyes they will think that I care – and of course I do. And I care to earn money and profit, and I care for the process with which the client process goes through – the experience that I bring them through; the whole experience of the initial meeting to the final delivery of product.

It has to be permeated with caring and effective communication. This is done again through questions – asking a lot of questions; positive, specific questions that have to do with them. This is an opportunity for you to make a positive first impression just by asking questions. If you're not sincere, by the way, you will telegraph insincerity. And for the most part, people can pick up on it. So if you have a hidden agenda, people will, just in their gut, get the wrong feeling about it.

And you may win some, and you may lose some, but it's not a game that I prefer to play the odds with. So, I'd rather increase my odds dramatically by trying to be very sincere, to be very focused and to be very centered. You know, when they're coming to you for photographs, really, it's important that they get good photographs. And it's very easy to stay on track with that as the end result, so all the questions ultimately are leading you towards that goal.

STAYING COMPETITIVE

This brings up a whole new area as well, and that is the idea of competing on price. This is a big question. When you're selling on price, I think you're making a real, real serious mistake. Selling on price is not the way to go. Even if people think they want to buy on price and price alone, oftentimes I can talk them out of it just by subtly and genuinely, and in time, through a progressive series of questions and demonstrations, show them why it's important to spend extra money to get good, quality value. But if all they want is just price and price alone, basically, I don't want to deal with them.

So, I have safeguards in effect to eliminate those types or those people from even approaching me. They slip by once and a while, and I quickly move on. But if I feel that they do happen into my life, and I have a chance of successfully converting them to not shopping just on price but to also shop on value and spend more money, then I'll do that. And I often succeed more times than not. But having a good price, has such a strong psychological effect on people, it is worth looking into.

Look at your prices. You want to be priced high enough, so that when people look at it they immediately make the equation – price equals quality. This is important; absolutely vital. If you think to yourself that you're selling effectively by pricing yourself at a bargain, then you're making a serious, serious mistake. Because you're going to end up with a lot of trouble, a lot of problem clients, and a lot of issues are going to be coming up. And it's going to be nothing but frustration. So look at your prices, first off.

KEY SALES TACTICS

Look at yourself. You know salespeople aren't born. I don't believe in that at all. I believe salespeople are made. Learning to sell is a skill, just like taking photographs, just like learning composition and lighting. For some of us, it's a little bit easier, we are predisposed. For some of us, it's a little tougher. But it's not something that is restricted to a select few people who have been ordained by diverse, divine intervention when they were born, it's in their DNA and all of a sudden they are without effort, they just evolve and grow into these incredible salespeople.

One thing that does happen is people who have a lot of enthusiasm become excellent salespeople. If you have enthusiasm on your side, you have one of the greatest gifts that you can use to effectively sell just about anything to anyone. However for most of us, that's not the case. But if you can get yourself to be enthusiastic, you can inflect enthusiasm into your sales process, into your personality, when you're presenting to prospects. You'll watch a wonderful thing happen. People just automatically click and will get on that bandwagon with you. And it'll help drive the sales process to completion effortlessly and quickly.

How do you become more enthusiastic? Easy question isn't it? Or is it? If you're not feeling very good, if you're down, you have to try and shoot for maximum energy, maximum enthusiasm. Shoot for maximum enthusiasm while you're in the process of speaking with clients, and if your enthusiasm starts to wane remind yourself to just bring it back up. And what happens in that case is you'll be going through like a rollercoaster, and that's okay. There's a natural forward motion, and that's all that matters. If you catch yourself getting down, keep moving onwards.

Now if you have a system in place, and you should have a system for selling whether you're trying to present your wedding photographs or other portraits, initial contact with clients, all your ads and marketing pieces, initial visit at the studio, the actual session itself, the return visit when they make their order and when they pick up. If you have a system in place for all these different areas, you're going to make your job a whole lot easier. So, that way you have the pre-described step-by-step way with which to get those things accomplished. But you want to avoid apathy. You really want to avoid where things become so routine for you that you start to become boring and dull and uninterested. So, it's important to build upon your system and maintain a pleasant, courteous, and enthusiastic approach. What you do to improve yourself, that's what you need to do.

If you're hiring staff to do it for you, you have to create a system, a system where you train your staff to go for as much courtesy and enthusiasm when dealing with clients as possible. And you must train them on a weekly basis, and reward them if you have to. Add incentives. But never, under any situation, should you allow for apathy nor should you allow for dullness to enter into the system. Don't assume that just because you trained them one time, that it's going to happen forever, unless they're naturally gifted and naturally enthusiastic.

But for most of us, we need to be reminded at a minimum, weekly. If you have an ongoing reward system where people are constantly looking for ways with which to remain enthusiastic and to remain at the very best top selling forum, all the better. You can do this by offering positive feedback, having a reward system based on you telling them they did a great job. Believe it or not, that process is far more important and far more effective than financial rewards.

But, hey, why not give both? Give them a tap on the back, recognize them for their efforts, do it on an ongoing basis, and give them some cash. And above all, live it yourself. So, don't take on the attitude of 'do what I say, not as I do,' because that won't work. When you have staff, you want to be seen as somebody who's a role model as well, because they'll be looking at you and mimicking whatever it is you're doing. This is very important. You must go first – professionalism in all areas of salesmanship, and you must go for consistency on an ongoing basis. So when you're selling, again, first impressions count. Who you are, counts. And having systems count. Having an effective pricing system counts. All these things work together. And being able to inform people also counts.

When I talk about the fact that selling is serving, I'm really saying selling is informing people. People come to you with a problem, and you have to offer solutions. And you do that by offering information. So every step of the process, you must be informing your clients at all times. Why do you use this particular mounting process? Why is that laminate that you use on your photographs good? What's included in your packages? What is retouching? How does the photographic session play out? When do I get to see the images? When are the images ready?

You know what I mean? These are simple, simple areas that we assume and take for granted. But when you take these areas and you put them into your sales process and you pre-emptively answer the questions, you're informing people. So, as you inform them, they are not only having their fears removed, but they are also liking you better because you're obviously somebody who cares.

They don't care about the fact that you've given that presentation a thousand times that year and that you've said the same thing over and over, and over again, because in their mind, it's applicable to them and their specific situation. They're coming in for a photographic session. And most of us, for the most part, have the same anticipation, and the same fears and expectations. So, when you answer a lot of these questions pre-emptively, you're speaking to most people. And again, they don't care that you've said it before. They think you're talking just to them, and you came up with it just for them. So therefore, now you have the connection with your prospect, and you're helping the process along.

PACKAGING YOUR PRODUCT

Part of having a good system is having a good presentation of packages. I'm a real big believer in having the three-tier packaging system. Essentially what I mean by that is silver, gold, platinum; or silver, gold, platinum, and platinum deluxe; or call it bronze, silver, gold, platinum.

The bronze package is essentially the economy package. It's basically the cheapest, the absolute cheapest you would want to go. But it's not really that attractive to the client.

The next package up is gold, which would be the target package. It is the one that you would want to have about 80 per cent of your sales towards, whether you're selling weddings, family packages, or baby packages. It doesn't matter. And you don't have to call these bronze, silver, gold, platinum. You can call them the basic package, the family package, the decorator package, or any of those other terms that we like to use in photography. Pick whatever one you want, it doesn't matter.

What's important is that you have your stuff in levels. People will look at the bronze, and say, "Ah, no. That's not . . . it's not enough." And besides, there's a real psychological issue that goes on, too. People don't want to be seen as cheap, so they oftentimes will not go to the cheapest package. They'll go to the package up or the package that is two up.

So if you have bronze, silver, gold, platinum, gold and platinum are the two target ones. Platinum plus or your highest priced package is your outrageously priced one. It's not really there to sell. You know, it'll be a very, very expensive package with just about everything in it. And it's there to put the gold and the gold plus, or the golden platinum packages into perspective. Its job is to look outrageously expensive. The economy package, the bottom of the barrel package, is there so that people won't buy it, and it prevents them from being too cheap. So they'll go to the middle. People are middle of the road. So price your packages accordingly – silver, gold, platinum or silver, gold, platinum, platinum plus.

Keep in mind that the two or one middle range packages are the target ones. And if it's not working for you, usually that means something else isn't working. Look deeper. But it's far more important to develop a system in time based on this idea so that you can use it over and over, and over again. And that is part of closing the sale.

When you go to close the sale, you have something. You can ask your client, your prospect, "Oh, have you heard about our family package or our heirloom package, which is ideal for people like you?" And they'll say, "Well, no I haven't, actually. Tell me more." Now you have the opportunity to explain to them. Now, what are you doing? Like I said earlier, you are informing them. You're not selling. You're not selling in the traditional hard sale approach. You're not grabbing their arm and twisting it behind their back and forcing them to make a decision against their will. That's not what this is all about. In a very patient, enthusiastic, loving and caring way, you are explaining to them what is in your package and why it is ideal for them. Let them decide that that is the choice they will make. It works.

When people ask you questions or raise objections, that is a very good sign. That means the sales process is moving forward. That is exactly what you want to have happen. If they are immediately closed off and they're confused, your sales process will be at risk of shutting down. But if they're asking questions, even if they're objections, this gives you an opportunity to answer those questions or to turn those objections into positives, simply by informing them. And you do this by knowing your product, knowing these questions in advance, pre-emptively answering them as much as possible or imagining scenarios where they . . . what could be the worst possible question they can ask, and have an answer that is based on that.

Often we make really good selling strategies work for us, and yet we fall apart when it comes time to ask for money. We sabotage the process. This is a common mistake with many photographers. It's easy to inform the client. It's even easier sometimes or if you use the right strategy, it's seemingly easy to get the phone to ring. And don't forget, selling is involved in the marketing, and it is a very large part of getting clients to the door.

So when you get them in the door and you start the sales process, you lead them right up to the very end, and then you sabotage. The main reason we do this is because we feel that either the client can't afford it, or we're overpriced, or otherwise we have some guilt associated with the high price that we are asking. This is a very important thing to try and get over. You have it clear in your own mind that the price that you're settled on is the price that you're going to stick with. And you're not going to make any judgments beyond that. Otherwise, you're going to be forever struggling and getting less than what you deserve for your product.

When you decide on that price, stick to it. If you waiver, if you start to falter, if they see you flinch, if you start to sweat when you quote the price, the process won't work. When you quote your price, you're essentially pitching them. After all is said and done, that's the final phase. For the most part, if you've done everything correctly, you'll get a very high closing ratio. Most people will be more than happy to pay the price. It may sting them a little bit, but if they look like they are little bit put off by your price, the worst thing to do is to start talking, because essentially, the next person who talks is the person who will own the prints.

So when you quote your price, don't flinch; stay steady and steadfast. Whoever talks next, buys the order. So wait until they talk – if they have an objection, if they have an issue, you can easily take it to that level and then resolve it.

WHEN TO BARGAIN

Another common issue that we see is people feel it's a little too expensive, and they want a bit of a bargain. I don't see a problem with that, and I do it regularly. All I do is make a package deal and take a little bit of a percentage off. No big deal. I mean it's still a good sale. Some ethnic groups are totally against paying anything other than cash in full price. And I will give them a package deal, as well. As a matter of fact, customizing packages is a great way to make the sale complete. Here's what I do often.

After a portrait sale, for example, or even for booking weddings, after we've chosen the pictures, the favourite photographs, say in a family shoot, I'll ask them, "What would be the ideal thing that you'd like? Tell me that and I'll create a special package for you based on the packages that I already have," because often the packages already have 100 percent of what they want in there. So, I'll get them in the process of choosing; and that's very important. They're already, in their minds, taking ownership by choosing which pose that they would like for their wall portrait and all the gift sizes.

Once I do all that, I list everything, I look at the package, I make slight modifications, and I definitely don't want to gouge myself or start to give everything away. That's a mistake. You don't want to do that. But I want to make it appear like I'm creating a package. And essentially, that's what I'm doing, because the packaging in and of itself isn't a reduced price from the 'a la carte' pricing. So, it's really the same thing. But in the client's mind, in their view, they see it as a special package just for them.

So, I list everything, create a special package price, and I'll write it out on my price list. I'll write it out in pen and with everything that's included in the package and show it to them. So when they see it in pen, with ink, on the paper, it helps to solidify. And most times they'll say, "Yes, that looks good. We'll go with that".

For a wedding of course, I do this before the booking is actually confirmed. This is before the actual wedding. So if they're shopping and I'm showing them my prices, I oftentimes will add a modification to the package, or sometimes I'll even throw in a free gift – maybe some five by sevens for the bridal party, or some other small add on. And it's just a standard policy in our studio that if that's what it comes to between myself and my wife, nobody's going to get in trouble by giving away a few extra goodies. And so we all have the discretion to do that. If we feel it is what is needed to close the sale.

TIME IS OF THE ESSENCE!

Another important factor that you have to be able to do and work into all your sales process is urgency. Urgency is very important. You have to have time limits placed on everything. This is so critical, I can't stress this enough. From your ads, to your sales pitches, and all your marketing pieces, having a deadline or time-limited offers – a sense of urgency is the fuel that will make things move along quicker than anything else. With a wedding booking, of course, you can do the same thing – add incentives, add a deadline. If you book right now, I'll throw in this, I'll throw in that. And with a family deal, family package, the same idea. Adding incentives to close the deal right away is a great way to speed the sales process along.

With proofs, if you let your proofs go, and this includes wedding proofs, controlling your sales process is absolutely vital to the success of your studio. Many photographers won't let their proofs leave the studio. And I don't believe any system is better than any other system; they both work as long as you work them properly. So when you do need the proofs, there has to be an urgency to get those proofs back – ideally, no more than five days because sales will begin to drop dramatically after five days.

As soon as the proofs leave the studio or leave your presence, immediately you start to lose control over the sales process. So it's important to have safeguards in place to make that happen. There has to be a sense of urgency. There has to be a time structure in order to bring them back to the studio. In our studio we ask for a substantial deposit. So, in other words, if they don't bring the proofs back, we keep the deposit. It's that simple. When the wedding proofs leave the studio, the whole package is paid for in full. So, theoretically, if we never see them again, their sale has been completed regardless.

We do want to see them again, in spite of that, because we want to create and maintain that relationship with clients, because a lot of our clients are repeat clients. As a matter of fact, over 80 percent of our clientele is repeat business. A long-term value of your clients is an equation that is worth considering in your entire five-year marketing plan, because every client has a long-term value. Five years is the average lifespan with which to consider their value.

So when you do let the proofs out and you do decide to do that, it's very important to put safeguards. If you are a higher volume studio with a lower price client, it's essential to never let the proofs leave the studio. It's integral to the process that you absolutely, under no circumstances allow them to leave the studio. In a higher end studio where you charge top dollar, I think it's perfectly acceptable for the proofs to leave the studio, as long as certain safeguards are in place.

Some of those safeguards are as follows: the client must be educated; you must have a good relationship with that client; they have to have paid a substantial deposit, generally a minimum of $200; there must be a sense of urgency; there must be scheduled time for them to bring them back; and if that does not happen, you must get on it right away and start calling right away, to reschedule a second time, a third time. So you must maintain control at all costs, at all times.

A lot of photographers will not let their proofs leave the studio. And that's okay, too. I'm not saying, like I mentioned earlier, one is better than the other. I'm just saying that if you do let your proofs leave the studio, you have to have safeguards. Now if you refuse to let proofs leave the studio, you are paying a price in one sense. In our studio I used to never let proofs leave the studio until I got so busy, I just decided that I couldn't stand all the time that it took to spend with clients, let alone the aggravation, and the fact that I had to tell everybody over and over again, "You don't get to take your proofs home; you have to choose right away," and all the objections. I would go through all that, but then because I got so busy, I just decided, "Hey, you know what? I'm going to start letting proofs leave, and I'm going to put in these new safeguards." And for the most part, I would say well over 99 percent of the time, it worked.

Now I know we would make more money if we absolutely maintained tight control on proofs and we never let them leave the studio. But I'm willing to pay that price for the freedom and all the extra hours every week that are allotted to me by letting the proofs leave the studio. I'm letting the system and the safeguards do the work for me. So when the proofs leave the studio, all those systems and safeguards are in place, including the education of the client. The client is educated on every aspect and I've almost planted seeds in their minds as to which package is going to be ordered and which images are going to be selected. So when that happens, the sales process is automated.

But again, you don't want to sabotage yourself and your selling. You don't want to get weak, especially towards the end when it comes time to ask for the money. We often do that. As human beings we tend to feel guilty. So you have to have confidence and strength. And you have to deal with the awkward feelings that come up when you're quoting your price.

SOME FINAL THOUGHTS ON SELLING

Selling is key to any business and to business success. And photography is no exception from the rule. We are not exempt from the importance of selling. So we might as well make it a key issue in our lives. We might as well learn the people skills that are required, and we might as well use the power of selling to achieve our financial goals. There's no other way around it. You have to incorporate selling into your life even if you think that you're an artist and that artists shouldn't sell. Well that is a fallacy as well.

Many famous artists throughout centuries have been very good salespeople. Salvador Dali, who is a famous modern painter who painted Surrealism, was a very astute businessperson, even though he was considered very artistic. Rembrandt sold hundreds, if not thousands, of paintings; and he had a real business going with his production. And opposite to that is Van Gogh. Van Gogh, who suffered most of his life and who literally died poor and penniless, had different values altogether.

Would you rather be successful and prosperous, or would you rather starve and associate starvation and poverty with pure art? The two should never be linked, as far as selling is concerned. Just because you're an artist doesn't mean you shouldn't be selling or you shouldn't learn how to sell. The commercial aspect to moving our portraits along and creating maximum business success and maximum profits in our lives is, without a doubt, of prime importance and essential to your development as a photographer and the growth of your photography studio.

CHAPTER 6

Marketing

"Effort only fully releases its reward after a person refuses to quit."

- Napoleon Hill, 1883-1970
(Author of Think and Grow Rich)

All business is based on a very, very simple economic fact – supply and demand. It's really that simple. You have something that people want. They are willing to pay you money for it. They're willing to trade their hard earned cash in return for that particular product and/or service. Then you have trade. You have an economic situation, an economic reality. If you think that just because you are a photographer with a specialized skill, or you have an "artistic" product that you do not fit in that simple equation, then you are fooling yourself, and you are in a state of confusion, and you are a perfect candidate for a serious wakeup call. Of course, the thing that drives the intensity with which that kind of trade will happen is marketing. It's all about marketing. Marketing is bringing your product to market. All the efforts, all the energies, all the actions, all the strategizing, all the thought processes and everything that goes into bringing your product or service to the market is called marketing.

A CAUTIONARY NOTE

Now there's a caveat that I always like to warn people about – and that is you need to have a good product. If you don't have a good product, then perhaps you're selling a lower end product on a higher volume. And there's really nothing wrong with that. But for the sake of argument, I'm going to assume most of us reading this book have a half decent product or better and are starting with something that will resonate with people in that respect, that they are out there with a minimal amount of quality. If you don't have a good product and you do have good marketing, you're only going to increase the speed with which the world around you discovers that you have a crappy product. It's a simple formula, again. But if you have a good product and you have good marketing, you have a very, very good chance of creating demand and trade, and a strong economic situation, and ultimately a good, comfortable business for yourself.

No business is immune to the process with which businesses have to evolve from. All the economic fundamentals, all the marketing fundamentals apply equally to photography studios as they do to butcher shops or jewellery stores, or any other merchant in any other industry or business, because that is very root core. We're talking again about supply and demand. We're dealing with human beings. And the thing that drives photography isn't so much a need that is based on necessity for survival, but it is a need that runs very deep for many of us, it is a vanity need, it is an egotistical need, it is in many cases, bragging rights as far as status is concerned – a nice portrait, very, very well created and crafted, of which in most cases was a fair size investment, that hangs in a beautiful home from a well to do family. That portrait is a status symbol in many cases.

But above and beyond all of that, a nice portrait is something that immortalizes our identities as individuals and as families. Not to sound too deep here or to get too philosophically involved in this argument, but just to touch on it briefly, there is a grain of truth in the idea that people want to eternalize and immortalize their presence on this planet. And having a nicely crafted portrait will do that, at least seemingly so, and will satiate that drive, that desire, and that hunger at least to some degree. So, all of these elements are the heart of the driving energy that creates a demand for us portrait studio owners.

But now back to marketing. Let's talk about marketing, because marketing, in my opinion, is the number one job. Without marketing you risk failure. If you are successful, but you say to yourself, "I've never really done much marketing." Well, if I looked a little deeper, I would probably discover that by default you probably were doing some marketing, you just weren't aware of it.

There were certain marketing elements that were working in your favour, and perhaps, you were at the right place at the right time. You were in a very fertile environment where it allowed you to virtually supply an unlimited demand for your services. And sometimes that's not a good thing, because when you struggle to create a business in a very competitive and a very demanding marketplace it hardens you. It makes you a better businessperson and a more strategic marketer. If you happen to grow your business with very little thought to the marketing process or the strategic process, well if that fertile ground is taken away from you, then you risk not knowing what skills you need to tap into or develop in order to develop a strong business.

Most of us, especially in today's day and age and today's economic climate where so many studios are noticing a dramatic drop in business, a dramatic decrease in the amount of volume that they've been doing, and there are reasons that we can speculate as to why that is, which I'll touch on briefly. But in today's day and age, we need to be more savvy. We need to be more in tune with the skill and mindset, and the talents that are required to be an effective marketer, because, in my opinion, being a marketer is the number one job.

I noticed a vast increase in my business when I started taking the marketing concept very, very serious. And it's not a coincidence that that was my best year, and every year afterwards. I incrementally grew my business by as much as 50 percent every year. But it didn't just happen. It had a lot to do with the fact that I really applied a lot of my time and energy to the job of marketer. This is not a new concept.

You've probably heard a lot of it said before, especially in the book by Michael Gerber by the title of *The E Myth*, where Michael talks about most business owners who are nothing more than technicians suffering from an entrepreneurial seizure. And he also mentions that, statistically, our odds of success are pretty dismal at best. And that in the first five years somewhere between 80 and 90 percent of businesses will fail. And after five years to ten years, 80 percent of those who succeed are going to fail as well. So he paints a pretty bleak picture. And it's not a hard picture to try and understand. All you have to do is look around in your own town or city. Look at the businesses that start up and in a year they're gone. They come and go. They're here today, gone tomorrow. So you don't want to risk being one of those numbers in your photography studio.

THINK MARKETER!

You really want to increase your odds by using strong marketing tactics, by applying yourself as a marketer. And when I say apply yourself as a marketer, I mean you really have to develop the skill set. You really need to develop those talents within yourself. Don't go looking outside of yourself. Don't try and throw money at marketing, hoping to get the answer from outside. The most common mistake I see in that area is where people hire a graphic designer, or an ad agency or a webmaster, or anybody who they think might offer the solution for them. The truth is, is that most of these people, in all likeliness, know way less than you do about selling your business at a profit, your services at a profit. How could they possibly? I mean, how can they know any more than you?

So if you develop the marketing and the strategic side of things, you will be able to apply that knowledge that only you have at such an intimate level. Now you might be resistant to this idea, but I would suggest to you to fight that resistance. Fight the urge, as Michael Gerber would say, to be a technician suffering from an entrepreneurial seizure, and develop the marketing mindset, develop the strategic mindset where you are a true entrepreneur and you are a true businessperson, and ultimately a marketer of photographic services.

I talk about this at great length in my marketing manuals and marketing system, and I can only really skim over it. But I think in this chapter, I can get the point through to you how important marketing is. And it's not something that you just decide to do, and next month you're good at it. This is a skill that takes years to develop. And the first thing, in my opinion, that you have to do is to set goals.

You have to set a five-year goal, a one-year goal, and a monthly goal. You have to know what markets it is you're after, what net profit you want to achieve in the next 12 months, and what volume you want to be achieving in the next five years. You have to get that clear in your head so that you have something to shoot for. And once you've got that clear in your mind, what you need to do is develop your time properly so that you're spending the majority of your time, in increasing amounts, working on the marketing side of things.

Let me give you an example. Awhile back when I first started becoming very aware of how important marketing was, I decided at that time to dismantle my darkroom. I had a great dark room with really nice equipment, and I took it all apart and sold everything because I had realized – and Michael Gerber's book, *The E-Myth*, really helped me realize this, at that time as well – I realized that I was spending too much time in the dark room. So that was one that I had done. I removed my chain that bound me to the dark room, and I outsourced that. And increasingly every month and every year since then, and that was many years ago, I have increased the amount of things that I delegated outside of my studio so that I can more and more, and more, just do the things that are so important to me. And that is ultimately, taking pictures and marketing.

There's a real bonus to this, too. And, again, I mention it in my marketing audio coaching tapes and in my manual. It's kind of funny, and there are probably reasons that explain why it happens, but as I became more of a business-minded person and an entrepreneur, and a marketer, I actually improved my talents. And I think there again, like I said, there are many reasons for it, probably because I did more business as I created more experience. But I think it's more than just that. I think it also has to do with the fact that I cleared out so many of the "technical" things in my studio that I was stuck doing. In other words, I was no longer a technician suffering from an entrepreneurial seizure.

I delegated everything, and it freed up my time so that I could take pictures and do marketing. And this allowed me to really get closer to my business to create more business. It made me a more prosperous photographer and businessperson. It allowed more sessions, and I got more experience, which has made me a better photographer. But because I wasn't dedicating so many hours a week to getting all that technical stuff done, it's almost magical. My talents increased as a photographer. My talents increased as a technician.

I hope you understand this point. I hope this point is really, really clear in your head that you must delegate everything in your studio that will not help you become a better marketer or a better photographer. You should be doing up to 90 percent of your time – that is the ultimate goal – up to 90 percent of your time should be dedicated to those two areas – marketing and photography. I'm not here to say that I'm at that level myself; maybe sometimes I come close to it. But you know what? Even if you are at 50 percent, you're doing way better than most people because most business people get so caught up doing the technical side of things that they never have a chance to fully realize what is really the top priority, and what is truly the important aspect, to creating a dynamic and a successful studio.

This is a huge leap for a lot of studio owners to get to. It is very difficult to absorb for many of us. But once you do, I can promise you that it'll bring you to bigger heights and better things, better business, and better photography. And I must say, too, that it would be scary, but there's a bigger responsibility, and perhaps that's the reason for the fear. But if you're not willing to take that responsibility that goes along with becoming a more successful and prosperous photography studio, then you're just not willing to be at that level. There's no way around it. More success equals more responsibility. You've just got to do it.

So don't get caught up on the technical side of things. Don't go to your studio and think, "Oh, I just spent six hours working on digital workflow. And now I'm applying myself. Look at how important I am. Look at how dedicated I am to my craft." That is wrong. In my studio, I don't do any workflow. It's 100 percent delegated. Well, I shouldn't say that. There's some that I do, but it's generally images that I want to take on out of personal desire and passion. And it's just my way of staying in that creative aspect. But for the most part, it's delegated. I have employees who do that, and they are properly trained. And we work very, very close with our lab. Everything is outsourced as much as possible, through employees or to services outside of my studio. I don't believe in printing in-house, although we do have a printer. It is there for emergency, last minute jobs, and for promotional items and whenever a particular need arises. We have an Epson printer that we use. Other than that, everything is delegated. I like to operate a lean, mean studio machine.

JUDGING YOUR PRODUCT

So how do you know if you've got a great photographic product? And if you're not too sure, there's a very simple way to find out. Don't trust yourself, and don't trust your mom. First of all, if you look at an image and feel that you're God's gift to photography, well, okay, maybe you are. Maybe you do really have a good product there. But if you're not sure, don't second-guess yourself, because we are likely our own worst critics or judges.

Don't go to your mom. Your mom will probably love you no matter what. I would go to a neutral person – maybe, just general people that are typically your prospects. Like, for example, if you have a child at a dance school that takes dance lessons. And you go there and there are other parents hanging around, and they all have children; there you go.

Just show them some of your images. Don't say anything. Just show them. And watch the kind of reaction you get. People will, by their reaction, tell you if what you have is crap or if what you have is very desirable. And it's usually pretty simple. It's an instantaneous thing.

There are many ways like that example, which you can use to try to tell whether or not you've got a good product. Sometimes all you've got to do is describe a product. Say if you're coming up with a certain idea, for example, the baby's first year wall panel is something that is very easy to describe – a portrait at all stages of a baby's first year. Most parents understand that. And if you have a good idea like that, or if you have an actual photograph to show somebody, a good response would be, "Oh, that's great. Where can I get something like that?" If you get a reaction like that, that's a pretty good indicator that you've got something that could potentially be a high, desirable item.

So let's assume now that you are no longer, in your mind, going to be stuck doing technical stuff. You're a marketer of photographic services and a photographer. You are capable of taking a fairly decent image and it is something that once you get it out there, there's going to be enough demand for. Where do you go from there?

Now we get a little bit technical. And I can again, only skim through those areas. But I think I can touch on them enough to really get the idea through to you. The marketing approach at this point and time that you need to take is nothing really new. And it is outlined in three steps – message, market, and media. Or as many marketing gurus out there like to call market, message, match. Now what is this? It's really simple. Your message is part of your product because for us photographers, we like to use our samples to promote our work. And so that is part of our message, obviously.

When a prospect looks at our work, they see what kind of work we do. If we were selling bread, milk, gasoline or any other commodity, the message would have to come through differently. But for us photographers, the message can come through visually and instantly because we are a visual medium. Now that's not the only thing. So don't get caught up in this belief that what I'm saying to you is that your photographs are your message, and that's it. There's far, far more to it than that. To assume that just because you can take a half decent picture, get a business card, hang out your sign on a shingle, and people are going to beat a path to your doorstep, is all you need to do, then you are taking a serious, serious risk at short-term success at best.

So your message is something that is well crafted from packaging and something that I like to call widgetizing. And that is, in my studio, I have created a lot of different programs based on gift certificates, based on time-sensitive offers, based on memberships – for example, the creative Kids Club membership, the baby's first year wall panel, the toddler panel, the sibling panel, the five year family plan – and newsletters that I send out on a regular basis with special time-limited offers again. These are all part of the message, and the message is nothing more than a description of what it is you have to offer. And the key word here is to innovate. You must innovate your message. You must have a way of packaging your message so it sounds different from everybody else out there.

A CLASSIC MARKETING MISTAKE

There's a common mistake that happens in virtually every industry, and photographers are not immune to this mistake – it is what some marketing gurus have come to term as marketing incest. And to talk about it briefly, I'll describe it. Marketing incest is typically a result of many people in an industry getting together on a regular basis, usually at conventions and conferences. And they end up talking amongst each other and looking at what each other is doing in their business in order to promote and market their businesses and studios. And they go home and they start doing the same thing, thinking that that's going to work for them, or that that is the reason for that other person's success. If you do this after enough years, it evolves to a very high level of ineffectiveness and a very high level of stupidity, which is a common by-product of incest.

So the antidote is to be innovative so that you stand out from all the competition in your area and that when you say something about your product or service, even if it's the same basic product at the same photographic skill level of many in your area, the way you say it, the way you craft your message will definitely give you an edge. And a lot of times this has to do with packaging and bundling. And it also is part of the selling process that is an important part, because if you don't sell your product properly, or if you're afraid to sell, then you're taking, again, another serious risk of failure.

REAL MARKETING KNOW-HOW

The second step that goes almost simultaneously or immediately right after your message is your market. You have to know the market you're after. If you have a very hungry market and you have identified them, and you have very weak marketing, you're probably going to do okay. But if you don't have a market, it doesn't matter how good your market team is, you're probably not going to get very far. So you want to go after a market that's hungry.

For me, and my studio, I decided to go after families, babies, children, and weddings. These are the markets that I targeted in my area and went after with a passion and a vengeance. And they're typical markets that many portrait studios end up going after. So, it's important to develop a strong sense of your market. Who are they? How do they think? How do they live? Where do they live? Where do they shop? What kind of activities do they engage in? What kind of associations do they belong to?

When I developed a sense of these answers, it really helped drive the message that I had created at that same time. It worked fabulously well, and I grew in more ways than just by business. I developed a whole new network of friends and associates, and not to mention all the new business that came my way. I joined new clubs. I started to become affiliated with new associations. And I started to cross-market with other businesses.

So you can see how if you strategically start to create your message and then you develop a targeted group of people that you're going to go after, there is without exception, no other way to really approach the development of your business and your business marketing plan. There is no alternate answer to the common myth that I hear often enough and that is when photographers tell me, "Oh that won't work in my area. Our people are different." Well that's nothing more than a load of lies. People are the same, generally speaking, everywhere. They have the same basic genetic makeup and same basic drive and ego, and perceived needs.

If you're looking for an alternate way, there is none. If you happen again to be successful, there's a really good chance that you have done a lot of what I'm talking about so far by default without even being totally aware of it. So target your market, develop a good sense of who those people are, but be brave, be bold and go forth and face them square on, eyeball-to-eyeball, nose-to-nose, belly-to-belly, and learn to sell to these people.

MESSAGE DELIVERED

The third step that is critical to this sequence is the media. The media is the method with which you deliver your message to the market. It is the method, whether it is technological, whether it is live and in person, whether it is by mass media, it is a delivery mechanism that brings your message to your prospect. And you can get very confused in any of these three steps just by allowing certain directions to take over, or allow certain technologies or misconceived ideas.

Some of the more popular ones are to throw money at, say, something very expensive like television ads. And you're thinking to yourself, "Well, I'm doing something because I'm spending all this money; therefore I am marketing." And then discovering eight months later that it didn't really work out the way you planned, and so you blame the system, instead of blaming yourself for making a stupid decision, for making an unwise move. You have to strategically approach all of these steps and not miss the final step – your selection of media. This is an easy one to get misguided on.

We can get totally sidetracked by the siren song of the ad agencies or we could become victims of the ad rep who comes in from the local newspaper and sells us a monthly or quarterly, or a yearly, plan of very expensive ads. Or worse yet, they sell us a very expensive plan, and they design all the ads for us. And the ads are nothing more than oversized business cards with the same results – nothing. And we end up with the same cynical view because it didn't work out for us.

We must be responsible in the selection and creation of our message, of our market, and of the media. And when you do this, you will see results. Some of my favourite media selections are displays, direct mail, and websites. Of course publicity and word of mouth are very important as well. But publicity and word of mouth are good once you've got your studio running and things are happening. You may be able to get some publicity if you have something very unique and innovative to bring to the local media that they can write an article on. But I wouldn't rely on that as the only leg that you're going to stand on, for now. It's always something to consider.

More importantly, when you target the people that you are going to go after, it's good to know where they live so that you can display in certain areas or stores that they shop in, or that you can send mailers to, or when you know what associations they belong to, you could do some cross-marketing with those associations.

I really drove my business to the level that I drove it to through those same media approaches. I would display in a shopping mall for up to two weeks prior to Christmas, but I had some really dynamic images to display. But I just didn't sit there and display everything; I also had a method for capturing names and addresses. I had a draw so that people filled in their name, address, and they check marked a little box that said, 'Would you be interested in receiving more information from our studio on special offers? Yes or No.' Most people would mark, 'yes.' And I also sold gift certificates, very, very actively at the display. So much so, that they ended up being a very high profit center for me.

Not only was I capturing the names and addresses of very, very hot leads, but also I was making money in the process. So the cost of putting these displays, which were typically very expensive because a good shopping mall doesn't come cheap, were often self liquidating, or I'd actually end up making money on the sale of gift certificates. And that's a really good way to get your name out there and get a whole bunch of names. And again, it's good if you have an established studio and you have some good images to show people.

THE GUERILLA APPROACH

If you don't have that, you might have to resort to more dynamic guerrilla marketing strategies. For example, what I did in my studio when I first started out was I created gift certificates that I placed in different jewellery stores. When somebody would buy a diamond engagement ring, they would get a free gift certificate for my studio. This got the phone ringing. This got clients in front of my camera. And of course I was able to up-sale them on further images, assuming I did a good job for them and assuming I created a nice portrait. I was not afraid to ask for another sale.

So there are many ways to get your name out there and get your phone ringing without spending a fortune. But you must be confident, and you must be willing to step out of the box and to go after them. You must go after them. If you think that going to an ad agency or spending money on expensive media is the solution, you have to take a good honest look at yourself and ask yourself, "Am I doing this because

I think that spending this kind of money is a way out? Or am I doing this because I'm really afraid or lazy to take the more effective road which is going to involve more dedication, more hard work, more facing of my fears?"

When you get out there and you shake things up, you just start a reaction that's, in many cases, almost magical. If you don't do anything or if you rely totally on ineffective media, you end up risking failure and cynicism. But if you just get out there and hit the pavement, especially when you're at the building stages of your business, you just start phoning people, you start making contacts, you start going out to meetings for different associations, whether it's Toastmasters International® or Rotary International® or any other type of association, be it the YMCA® or Lions Clubs International®, any other group of that nature, you start a reaction and the universe starts to move with you. So if things are not working out, generally, there's another issue that you have to take responsibility for.

There's another issue that you have to seriously look inwards at yourself for, and start at square one. Look at, like I mentioned earlier, your product. Is your product good enough? Don't fool yourself in this area. Do you have a marketing plan? Does your marketing plan own the three basic steps that you need to follow? In other words, do you have a good message? Do you know who your market is? And are you using effective and responsible and measurable media, such as direct mail, such as affiliations with other businesses and associations? Or are you looking at putting up displays?

BECOMING DEAN OF THE DATABASE

When you build your business, the most important asset, and it is going to be the most important marketing tool available to you, is going to be your list of and your database of clients. Assuming they are satisfied, happy clients, they will come back to you on a regular basis. And they will tell all their friends and neighbors about you. This is a goldmine. From the first client you get, you should be recording their names, addresses, phone numbers, and emails. And you should be considering keeping in constant touch with them on a regular basis.

The ideal situation is to be in touch with them no more or no less than once month. If you can't, do that, shoot for at least four times a year – once every season. How do you do this? Through newsletters, through postcards, and through sales letters. Whatever it takes, send them something. Let them know you appreciate them. Send them something interesting and entertaining, and make dynamic offers. This group is a far more important targeted group than any other group you have available to you. Once you develop a list – and it starts generally when you get a good list of about 500 – you'll notice results. And even if you're only at 100, you should still start the process and start the habit of keeping in touch with them on a monthly basis or every three or four months. It's a good habit to get into.

Do they all have to be previous clients? Not necessarily. Anybody who's expressed an interest in your business will be in this database. Mind you, you can break up your database into 'A' list, 'B' list – 'A' list being all of those who have purchased from you, and 'B' list being all those who have expressed an interest in purchasing from you. It's an idea worth considering if you'd really like to fine tune the database management strategy.

What I would recommend you do, is if you put on displays and you capture leads, or if you belong to an association . . . and for example, I was in Rotary, and I developed in Rotary a little mini project where I was going to, through a fund-raiser, purchase a camera for the Rotary club because I noticed that they always wanted pictures every week or every two weeks, when somebody was receiving an award.

But I couldn't be there all the time and nor did I necessarily like the idea of me being the guy who's taking all the photographs. And so I thought, "Well, why don't I get a camera for the club," one that anybody could pick up; and it was a basic point and shoot camera. So I pitched it to the club, and said, "Listen, let's have a fund-raiser for a new club camera . . . I'll put up some little packages for sale, and they'll be for sale for a limited time only." And typically that was a session with a reprint, and all the monies collected from those went 100 percent to the purchase of a camera.

So what I had done, I don't remember the exact figures, but it was something in the idea of around $50 for a designer portrait session. At that time, my designer portrait sessions were $100, so it was a very desirable offer because it was 50 percent off. And all the people who purchased the gift certificate ended up going in my database. So there was like 20 or 30 names on some very, very hot leads. And the club ended up with a nice, new camera. And I looked like I was the good guy.

Not only that, when I promoted these gift certificates that I used as a fund-raiser for the Rotary club, I brought actual samples to the meetings to help promote the sale of these gift certificates-fundraiser. I would have a table set up at a few of the meetings with my sample portrait. It was a wall portrait on a nice easel. And you could go there and sign up your name. I got to promote to the entire club, and everybody knew me through my little mini camera fund-raiser that I'd put on, they got to see the kind of work that I'd done.

So it was a win-win situation, and an excellent way to help build my business. All the names that I collected from displays in malls, you could collect names from displays in restaurants or grocery stores or hair salons. There are so many places with which your prospective clients, your targeted group of those most likely to buy from you, where they will shop at, that you could hit up and do some cross promoting with, and start creating a list of names to put into your database. And that database and the relationship that you created with those people is the most valuable asset in your business because you can go back to them over and over, and over again and sell to them.

The money that you spend on marketing to that group of people is money that is going to be very, very well spent because you're not going into it blind; you're not going into that marketing arena wondering whether or not the money is going to bring you any kind of return. You know these people are going to buy from you because they bought from you before, assuming you didn't do a lousy job or that they're not mad at you for some other reason.

But let's assume they're pleased as punch with you, there's a very good chance they will buy from you again or that they will promote, say for example, a referral gift certificate program that they can offer to their friends or relatives. They will do this for you because they have a strong relationship, a strong bond, with you. The money on the marketing and all the energy you put towards marketing to that group of people is money well spent. Why would you want to go out there and try to reinvent the wheel? Why would you want to go out there and try and market to new people and try to find new prospects all the time? You're eventually going to hit a brick wall, and you're eventually going to drive yourself to a very high level of frustration.

Recognize the fact that your past clients are your most valuable targeted people. Hold them close to you, hold them dear to you and treat them right. Get them on your side. They will be your allies, and they will help you grow your business stronger than anything else. And use the methods with which you market to those people in very innovative and creative ways.

THE ART OF MAKING NEWS

In my opinion, nothing is better than a marketing newsletter where you get to send out a four- or six-page newsletter loaded with offers and newsy tidbits and advice. And some of you may be thinking or you have heard others who have said that that kind of marketing doesn't work well. If you were noticing it doesn't work, I would dare to say that it's not working for you because something in it or something in the process is not working for you. Fix that something and you'll notice that newsletters work like gangbusters.

How do you make them work? Very simple, send them something that's very interesting that they will find very fascinating. If you send them something that's very corporate, very sterile, of course they're not going to like it; they're not going to read it. You're not going to send them something that's not going to produce very good results. You want to send them something that is written in a very conversational style that is quirky and fun. Typically, you want to really write about the non-studio related stuff. You want to talk about other stuff. You could talk about goings-on in your life, you can highlight newsy items that are adventurous that have to do with your community – whatever. Make it interesting though, and make it conversational, and speckle your newsletter with dynamic offers and credibility builders for your studio.

Marty Rickard was a photographer that I had long admired and who had a monthly article in the PPA magazine. He once said that if you tickle the earth, it would spring forth a bounty. What he means is get out there, rattle a few cages, and make your presence known. People are generally fascinated by photography. Although the genie is out of the bottle because of digital photography and photography is more accessible now than ever before, the photographer who is able to craft a very high impact portrait will always be admired and respected by his community and peers. And when you run out into the community and you show up with that, and you combine that with some very high-powered marketing, you are destined to succeed without a doubt in my mind.

But if you tuck yourself away, hold yourself up within four walls and expect the world to come beating a path to your doorstep, you're nothing more than a sad story; a disillusioned cry-baby. Cynicism and being of the attitude that the world owes you a living, or what I like to call having an attitude of entitlement. It's reserved for children and adults who don't know or have the ability to take responsibility.

When you think the world owes you a divine right to business and it owes you a living, then you are not going down a progressive road that will evolve into a more dynamic state. You know, with business people, I really, really believe that a business is an extension of ourselves and that through good, effective marketing that we get to develop and grow our business. And in turn we evolve as better people.

If we become cynical, negative, and disillusioned, I firmly believe we took the wrong path. Even if we are successful financially, we're not going down the right road. If we are successful and achieving success in a balanced way, we become better people and we become more of who we are meant to be. And it's a wonderful thing. And I believe it's the destiny that we can all become a part of, if we allow it to happen. We have the power in our own minds to decide what it is we want for ourselves. To look outside to externalize for answers, or to externalize for excuses is going backwards.

The four walls that we can enclose ourselves and cocoon ourselves in is a metaphor for taking the wrong road. You want to take a road that's open and that is full of creativity and prosperity. Even if there's more responsibility, more social, personal and community responsibilities, it is a better dynamic. It makes you a stronger, better person. And it all ties in with owning and growing your own photography business.

YOUR PERSONAL LEARNING CURVE

You know school is never out. As a marketer and as a photographer we are always, always learning. It is so important that we keep honing our skills on an ongoing basis so that we can keep up with the times and that we can keep up with the demands. If we get stale, we have no one else to blame than ourselves. If we think we are entitled for whatever reason, then we are developing cynicism; and you want to avoid that. You want to constantly be open and constantly be progressing. And the one way to do that is to constantly be experimenting and learning and prospering.

You can't do any of that if you're stuck as a technician or if you're stuck as Michael Gerber would say, doing it, doing it, doing it, doing it, doing it. All day long, week after week, doing it, doing it, doing it. Caught up in the "doing" of your business. You want to get away from the "doing it" and get into the growing of it so that you can achieve success with prosperity and develop a system for success, because marketing is a system. And the system that I firmly believe is the only system is the one that I've outlined in this chapter, and that is following the message, market, media approach. And constantly working those angles all the time so that they are always evolving and you are becoming more aware of them on an ongoing basis, which will in turn, make you a more talented marketer and in tune with the demands of the marketplace, and a more successful photographer.

CHAPTER 7

The Business of Running Your Business

"Our problem is not that we aim too high and miss, but that we aim too low and hit."

- Aristole, 384-322 BCE
(Greek philosopher, student of Plato and teacher of Alexander the Great.)

Taking photographs and making a profit is a business. Creating something that is sellable is all about creating something that people want. This is pretty simple to understand, but it's where we all have to start. If you're doing business or trying to create a demand based on anything else, you won't end up with any business. It's a hard and cold reality, but it's a reality that most successful photographers embrace, the fact that we are in a business. Your soul purpose is to make your business efficient and profitable. Beyond that, what you do with your life and the money that you make is up to you; it's a personal decision. But you have to start off with the right mindset, not with some distorted and idealistic view of the world.

In this chapter we're going to talk about some practical aspects to running your business. There is one thing you have to do, and that is to keep an eye on the chequebook. That is the one activity that you should not delegate. You should be watching where your money goes all the time. As well as, you should be watching all the money that comes in. What you measure, you improve. And this counts for expenses and income. And when I'm talking about income, I'm not talking about the gross. Ultimately, it's about the net. It's a common mistake with many to look at the gross and think they're doing okay. It's your pre-tax net that counts. What are you taking home? That's what really matters.

But keeping an eye on the chequebook is critical. Who are you writing cheques to and how much money you're spending month-to-month is very, very important to keep an eye on. It doesn't mean that you have to do all the accounting. As a matter of fact, I think if you're doing the accounting, you're making a great mistake. Perhaps it's okay at first, but as soon as you possibly can, and probably sooner than later, you ought to be looking for ways to delegate all the accounting activities so that you can remove yourself of that gruesome activity.

I don't care if you're really good at accounting and you understand bookkeeping. You might even have a degree or a diploma as an accountant. You should still delegate it so that you can do the things that we talked about in the previous chapter – the marketing and the photography. You'll get caught up. And don't try and rationalize or find ways to justify these grunt activities. And again, the only exception is watching the chequebook. You must sign all the checks and watch your money all the time. Keep a close, watchful eye on them. I'm not talking about white-knuckling it and penny-pinching to the ninth degree. I'm just talking about keeping an eye on things so that you know where it's going.

KEEPING AN EYE ON THE PRIZE

Another area of running your business is in your goal setting. It's important to not aim too high. If you make your goals unrealistic, if you make your objectives beyond what you're capable of, it will discourage you. It's important to have a five-year plan, but it's also important to break it down into a one-year goal and break it down into a monthly goal – something that is achievable and something that will allow you to stretch a little bit.

I've seen photographers who set their goals way too low; they go the opposite direction. And that is a serious mistake, as well. You have to achieve enough money to have financial freedom to buy you all the things and to have no debts, to be able to live a very wholesome and healthy life. All too often we associate that lifestyle with some sort of evil profiteering, money-grubbing personality. But that's not the case at all.

So, just like aiming too low, you cannot aim too high. You've got to set your sights realistically. I put that in this chapter because it is a practical attitude that we must have. It is not an area of being motivated or being . . . but it's a practical area where we have to keep a realistic eye on the monthly goals that we want to achieve.

TEAM BUILDING

Let's talk about employees for a second. Employees are critical. Putting together a good team that will help you grow your business is essential. For many of us, especially for small studio owners who start out as either 'mom and pops' or as individuals, it's often a challenge to break out and start hiring somebody. There are some common mistakes that we make when we start getting into hiring employees. I'm going to talk about a few of them right now.

One of the things that people do is they become too friendly with their employees. When you become too friendly with your employees, you lose sight of what the true relationship is supposed to be. I'm not saying to be a mean, demanding boss, but there has to be a bit of space between you and your employees. You should take good care of them, but you should also keep focused on business and the effective running of your business. It's a common mistake. That's why I'm bringing it up.

People get too close to their employees and they get to treat them like friends, and their employees end up taking advantage of them, productivity goes down, they walk all over them. They lose respect. And you don't want any of that happening. You want to stay focused on what is important and what is critical. I've learned a lot of this from experience. I've learned that it's important to spell out exactly what it is that your employees need to do, and set regimented times with which to get them done, to allow for proper training, and to allow for productivity to reach it's maximum.

It's also a good idea to find a way to give incentives to your employees – gifts, monetary gifts, recognition; these are all good areas. Studies have proven that employees value positive feedback far more than anything else. They value when you praise them and recognize them for a job well done. So recognition, in many ways, is probably one of the most important attributes to effectively working with your employees.

Employees are valuable because they do the things that you are going to delegate, that you are not going to do, so that you can become who you are destined to become, so that you can become the best photographer you can become, and you can become a master marketer of your business. You can delegate everything else to your employees. It's daunting for many of us to work with other people this way. And it's tricky for many of us when we're first trying to choose an employee.

Let me give you some suggestions that I've learned for picking employees. One of the things that I've found to be a really great way to streamline the process of choosing the best employee is by placing an ad in the local newspaper. I might run three ads throughout one week if it's a daily newspaper, every second day. And the instructions will be very, very clear in the ad. The instructions will outline what it is I'm looking for and outline what I need them to do in order for them to apply.

Typically, it goes something like this: "Photography studio looking for office help. Enthusiastic and outgoing people. Fill out and fax a one page, handwritten letter to . . ." And then I'll put my fax number. Why am I doing this? First of all, I don't want to see resumes. I want to see faxes, handwritten. And those who are too lazy to follow that simple set of instructions, I've immediately weeded them out anyways. So if they are willing to go and fill out a fax, one page, at least I know they've passed that initial criteria. And I can look at their handwriting. A person's handwriting will tell you a lot about themselves. And I'm not being specific about what it is I'm looking for, so they get to be creative and write out whatever it is they want. So if a person really sells himself or herself, that's a good sign. If they are genuine, it should come out in that one page letter.

Now, what you want to do is put out a pile of prospects, and then those that you're not interested in. So, if all goes well, you should end up with about 15 to 30 faxes. The ones that catch your attention are going to be the ones that you're going to call back and you're going to set up interviews. As a rule of thumb, we have generally found that we end up interviewing about six to eight people. During the interview process, it should become self-evident as to who is going to be a good employee for you.

I should mention here at this time, if you know a friend who knows a friend, or a relative who is interested in the job, that just because they're your friend or relative, it doesn't mean you should hire them. A lot of people think that getting the job is a matter of 'who you know'. But you don't want to fall into that trap unless you are totally convinced that they are the right people for the job. You'll make enemies quicker by getting involved in this kind of a relationship when it's not a good fit to begin with. So you want to make sure it's a good fit.

GETTING TO THE HEART OF THE MATTER

When you start the interview process, some key things to watch out for are a person's desire. If they have a strong desire for this position, if they are hungry for it and they truly want to be a part of your establishment, this should come out in the interview. They'll say things. They'll have a sparkle in their eye. You'll just have a good feeling about them. These are important things to watch out for because you want to hire the right person. What you do is ask impromptu questions.

I don't like following a strict order when it comes to trying to find the right employee. There's just some very generic questions, like, tell me a little bit about yourself; tell me a little bit why you think this is a good job for you; what are your plans for the future; where do you see yourself in five years? If you ask generic questions like that, you'll get to the heart and soul of a person.

Frankly, I had no desire or very little desire to look at their prior experience and qualifications, unless it directly applies to the qualities and characteristics that I'm looking for. And these characteristics are enthusiasm, desire, and teachability. I don't care if they've got years of experience on certain word processing computer software. I don't even care if they're super well established with PhotoShop. If they meet the other criteria, they will be a good fit. That's been my experience.

When I'm hiring somebody to do workflow – in other words, they're going to be sitting at the computer all day long – I try to avoid photographers. I find photographers are a bad fit because photographers generally don't want to sit in front of a computer all day. This should be obvious to most of us, but it's not. We think that, 'Oh, we're a photography studio. We're doing workflow, hence I'm going to hire a young, beginner photographer to come in'. The fact is, they're going to go crazy sitting at a computer all day. So I always look for somebody who has a predisposition to working at a computer all day.

People who are and have worked at video editing are a good pick, or perhaps even people who have done PhotoShop® workflow jobs in the past. Oftentimes these people need to be retrained and refocused on the system that I've created. And the system that I've created to that particular position is probably a lot different than what a lot of photography studios have done in their own establishments. So I have to retrain them and reprogram them to do exactly what it is I need them to do to get our workflow done.

Our workflow, by the way, is very simple. We have streamlined it to the point where we are maximizing the use of our time and ultimately, we are maximizing our profits and the bottom line. Graphic designers or graphic design students are another good choice because they typically sit at computers all day. Although they may find it a little bit cumbersome and boring after a while. Either young students or recently graduated students are good choices, as well, from the graphic design programs because they are eager to get as much experience as they can. So they are worthwhile considering.

THE QUICK SWORD APPROACH

When you find yourself in a position where you have an employee and it's not working out, oftentimes we as employers are the last people to come to the realization or at least come to the point where we finally decide to take action. It's a good idea to remember the philosophy behind the quick sword. And that is as soon as you know there's a problem, if you really want to help your business along, use the philosophy of the quick sword. In other words, get rid of the problem as soon as you possibly can.

Don't lollygag and don't wait and hope that things are going to change, that things are going to get better, or that a person's behaviour is going to get better. You'll only end up driving yourself crazy. If you sincerely think that there's a chance that improvement could happen, you can have a discussion with your employee and consider that somewhat of a warning to them. You don't have to tell them it's a warning, but you know in your own mind and heart that if you have to sit down and refocus them and have a heart to heart talk with them, that really you're keeping a close eye on them and that if they don't change, if things don't improve, then you're going to take immediate quick action.

If you apply this philosophy, you're doing something that most business owners don't do. And so, you might as well be brave, be bold, be different, and above all, be efficient. So get rid of waste as soon as you possibly can so that you can get on to being productive. Why would you want it any other way?

You know in business we have to take off our rose-coloured glasses.

We have to be able to look at things very, very objectively. We have to be able to take all aspects of running employees, and accounting, and the marketing, and everything that is to do with making our business as effective and as profitable as we possibly can. We have to look at it very objectively. Many photographers and photography studio owners are predisposed to putting on their rose-coloured glasses and having an unrealistic, filtered view of what is going on around them. This is why I feel it's so important to put up a five-year plan.

Know where you want to be in five years. And have something that is worthwhile going after. When you have that, that will be your guideline, that will be your map, that will be your destiny with which you get to focus on. When things are thrown in your path and you don't know what to do, then you can always fall back on, 'Well this is where I want to be in five years, therefore, I have to take this action and that action because these things are not helping me or they need to be modified'.

SWEEP THE SIDEWALK

I have an uncle who successfully ran a hardware store for many, many, many years. And his philosophy was, sweep the sidewalk. In other words, if you drove down Main Street where his hardware store was, his place looked good. The first thing that people saw when they looked at his hardware store was a very clean and a very inviting place. There wasn't any dirt on the sidewalk. There was a lot of merchandise out in the front, properly placed, uncluttered, and on display. We have to take the same philosophy in our own businesses, whether we're operating a storefront, or whether or not we're operating a home studio.

What people see when they first pull up is important. And I would be so bold as to further that principle to all areas of our life. Look at your closets, look at your car, look at your garage, your shed, your basement, look at all your storage areas, look at your office. Is it cluttered? Is it full of stuff piled up here and there and everywhere? How often do you see that type of situation in other people's lives? If you have clutter and chaos in any way, shape or form, you are creating a barrier to prosperity. So it's important to 'clean the sidewalk' and to clean all the sidewalks in your life. Have a nice, organized, clean, well-placed, systematized spot for everything. And keep it that way. You have to maintain this; not just do it one time and then let it, over the month, evolve into another state of chaos. You have to be vigilant in cleaning the sidewalk.

Even if you have a very clean and a very respectable look, if you're still cluttered behind the scenes, that's not necessarily a good thing because it usually represents more barriers even though your prospects and clients who come up to your place of business can't see that. It usually means there is still clutter going on. And the clutter I'm also talking about is clutter that has to do with deeper issues or psychological issues, or a reflection of how dirty our sidewalk is or how cluttered our lives are. If we are loaded with debt, that's clutter. If we have some addictions, that's clutter. So as you can see, there are many dimensions to clutter in your business starting from deep within yourself, all the way out to your physical environment with which you work in. So, it's important to have a look at all these areas so that you can clear it out and open the way to total prosperity and total success.

TALKING ABOUT TIME

Let's talk about time management for a bit. Time is very important and often an area that most of us would rather just as well not talk about. Time management can be a very dry and boring subject. If you've ever taken a time management course, it's not the most exciting thing to talk about. But still is a very important and critical success principle behind the proper use of time, because your time is your time. We are all given the same exact amount of hours per week, and what we do with that time will ultimately be reflected in what it is we achieve in our businesses and our lives. So it's very important that we talk about and discuss at a deeper level the use of time.

I'm a big believer in regimenting my time. I know that sounds scary, and it sounds like you're in the army. But by regimenting, I simply mean I allow time throughout the week for certain activities. For example, Monday to Friday, I have, in my life, time slotted in my agenda and I have this printed out so I can see it in my office all the time. And I can be reminded of what it is that I'm trying to properly do with my time.

So, I would suggest that you start by writing out the seven-day agenda and simply write out the things that you're going to do minimally every day that you're going to dedicate to. So, for example, on Monday at night between 8:00 and 10:00, you could be doing marketing. And on Tuesday, between 8:00 and 10:00, you could dedicate to a self-improvement course. And on Wednesday, same time, you could be dedicating it to the writing of your studio newsletter, etc. So you can see where, if your regiment certain hours a day, every day, but keeping in mind, and for me it was on weekends, where I would not regiment anything because those were family times. But typically, for Sunday night to Thursday night, I would regiment hours that I would do minimally dedicated to activities that were important to the success and growth, and productivity of my photography studio.

Again, I remind you, simply thinking about it is not a good idea. Sit down and actually write this out. And then print it out so you can physically see it with your eyes, and it'll give you a whole new objective, which you commit in pen. It makes a big difference when you write it out. You are making a step towards realization. Throughout the rest of the week, the time during the studio operations should be regimented towards all the other things I've discussed in this book so far, and that is effective use of your time so that you are doing the things that are going to bring you clients, and most productive and most profitable results.

A lot of studio owners want to have their weekends off, therefore they won't shoot weddings. And that's okay if you choose to do that. Weddings aren't as evil as a lot of photographers cut them out to be. For some oddball reason, a lot of photographers associate weddings with working late into the night Saturday, and then putting in another 30 to 40 hours throughout the rest of the week. Well that's not the way I run my wedding business. And I am very successful at the amount of weddings that I photograph, and the results that I get from them. In my studio, I'm home at, the very latest, 7 o'clock on Saturday night. And afterwards, I will put in an additional, personally, four hours of workflow.

I like to workflow my wedding images because I get a big thrill out of doing that. All the work that goes into the wedding images afterwards is done by my staff. But frankly, there isn't that much to do, because none of our packages include albums. When we do have albums that are sold and they are sold 'a la carte', I don't create them myself. So I've created a system of getting my wedding workflow done efficiently, and I make decisions that are based on that idea. It confounds me to no end why some photographers' workflow their images the way they workflow them. They end up spending 40 to 60 hours on every wedding because they work on each and every image, and they make sure they're absolutely perfect. Or they insist on and include albums in every single package, giving the bride and groom no other choice.

My wife likes to call wedding albums a "photographer's vanity". In other words, in her opinion, she feels that it's more important to a photographer that an album be put together; and oftentimes this is true. The products that we deliver to our clients are slide shows, DVDs, image catalogues, and such – things that are a different way of presenting images and that do not require the use of productive album creation. So that's one way that we effectively use and manage our time.

We sort of dictate how it is we're going to shoot weddings, not letting the client make those decisions for us. I hope you follow me on this one and understand what it is I'm trying to say. It takes a certain amount of confidence and it takes a certain amount of balls to be able to say to a client, "No, we don't do that. This is the way we do it." But you have to have a good, solid belief in yourself and a good solid product in order to back it up. And I like to use weddings as an example because it is an area that for many photographers, they somehow associate a lot of frustration and/or disdain with. We've created a system around weddings that makes sense for us and then we've sold our clients on that system pointing out the features and benefits and what not. We have to run our time the way we run everything else in our lives and our businesses. We want to have an uncluttered, clear, clean, working environment with which to start from. And this also involves the proper use of our time.

If you're spending too many hours in front of the TV every night, that'll be reflected in your ultimate success. Likewise, we can go the opposite way and end up just doing nothing but work, ignoring our families or our social networks. We have to strive for balance and put things in proper priority as well. And time management and the proper use of time and the way we schedule our week-to-week activities is important in helping resolve this.

A great use of our time as well is in our communities. It's my opinion that it's important to dedicate a certain amount of time to the benefit of our community so that we can contribute back into our community. This may be harder at first, but as you succeed and prosper more, you will be able to allow yourself to give more of yourself to your community. It's one thing to fork over dollars to the community and non-profit efforts, but it's totally something else to contribute hard time and talent.

Another area, too, is to allow a certain amount of time for self-improvement. We should be constantly growing and learning and reading and studying. So, a self-education program is essential. Even if we only allow one to two hours a week, at least do something so that you're continuously expanding your mind and you are continuously growing as a business person and as a photographer. I have noticed over the years that the most successful business people are the ones who can't get enough. They're always looking to improve in small ways. They're always looking for new and more exciting ways. They're always on fire; eager to learn; eager to grow. Why not be like them?

THE SWIFT SWORD REVISITED

I talk about the swift sword philosophy, which is a philosophy that applies to many areas. In your photography studio, if something isn't working, cut it off. If a particular area that you were hoping to go after and create a new market for, and if it's going to become a new income stream for you, and it's just not working, and it's more hassle than what it's worth, cut it off. Do it quickly. Move on to bigger and better things.

Sometimes it's not worth the pain and agony and aggravation to try and breathe life into something that's just ultimately going to drive you crazy. It's a reflection as well of you and who you are as a person and your ability to say 'no' or your ability to stand unflinching with confidence as you quote your price, really is what your business is all about and where it all starts. Truly successful people are immune to criticism. Not only do they have all the other things going for them that we talked about in this chapter, but deep inside themselves they have the knowing, strong confidence that they are worth the money that they are asking.

WHAT YOUR BUSINESS SAYS ABOUT YOU

The running of your business is ultimately a reflection of you. The business of running your business, every aspect, everything that we've talking about so far, is reflected upon what it is that you truly believe in yourself. So, really when I'm talking about the running of a business and all things management, all things delegated, all things that are leading to profit, all things will all stem from and radiate from who it is you are. If you want to be a good manager, become a good person.

If you want to become a good photographer, become a good person.

If you want to become a good marketer, become a good person. Start from a good set of values deep within yourself. These things are not things that start or that you'll find from an external side of yourselves. These are things that start from deep within and radiate outwards. Your ability to be confident and radiate success starts within yourself. So, when something is thrown your way, you're not thrown off course. When somebody criticizes you, you don't have an emotional reaction. You are able to stay focused and be resilient because you can focus on what it is you are trying to achieve for yourself.

There are examples all around. You don't have to look far to know what it is I'm talking about. All you have to do is look at businesses that are very successful, and look at businesses that aren't, and you'll know exactly what it is I'm talking about. And you can apply these exact same examples for success or for failure – the choice is yours – in your own photography business.

CHAPTER 8

The Art of the Pose

"Your work is to discover your world and then with all your heart give yourself to it."

- Siddhārtha Gautama
(Supreme Buddha, founder of Buddhism)

Why would anybody want to talk about posing, and dedicate an entire chapter to it? Why not? So, let's go for it.

I feel that posing is such an integral, important part of photography – especially for portrait photographers – that it's a worthwhile subject to dedicate all this talk to it. It's an area that I've noticed, especially for a lot of photographers, even those who have been around for many, many years, and likewise many who are starting out, there's still a level of lack of mastery and amateurism that comes along with posing. Posing, I feel, is very important to the creation process. It's a stepping-stone to the final product, the final image.

But there are certain things that need to be talked about and opened up and aired out. Mainly one of which is when you start posing somebody, you're at a level of confidence that you radiate to your client. And how you communicate and your inner calm is essential, and a direct link to how you pose them. What you have to know, first of all, is how it is you're going to have them looking in the shot before you can actually pose them. When you pose a subject, you have to know by not getting there through stumbling and fumbling. You have to master the basics.

There are many courses in which they talk about feminine posing, masculine posing. I was fortunate enough in my lifetime to have spent almost four years photographing school pictures, where, although there's a downside to doing the same assembly line approach to photographing hundreds and hundreds of kids every week, I still, never the less, really developed a strong sense of the anatomy and strong idea of what a good masculine and a good feminine pose is all about.

If you want to get to that point, you want to be able to look at a person and through a very minimal amount of interaction with them, and the proper use of light and exposure, make it all come together effortlessly. It has to appear effortlessly. And painlessly for the person being photographed. I notice many photographers who, even some who are teaching, seem to struggle or are only halfway there in this area, that it's not effortless.

For example, it drives me crazy when somebody is photographing and posing, say a family or a couple, and they go to the camera, and the lights are all set up, and they do their initial pose. And to me it looks good, and yet they're just about to take the picture, and they stop and they go back, and they adjust, or they give out another set of instructions. They ask the dad to turn his whatever, and they just start tweaking. And it drives me crazy. That would drive the subject crazy if they were being photographed and then there was this constant stop and go, stop and go, stop and go. Don't get behind the camera and start taking the photograph and then stop, until you're ready to get behind the camera and take the picture.

Sometimes you're better off just taking the picture and skipping the whole process of fine tuning, fine tuning, and more fine tuning when it becomes a constant series of aggravation, and stop and go. This is a part of posing that many of us lack and we need to get better at it. The only way you can do it, is through experience. The more you photograph people and the more you practice what it is I'm talking about, the better off you'll be at it. And the more mastery you'll have over these skills.

POSING AND ZEN

Posing is intuitive and at the same time, it is structural. It has to happen in a Zen-like fashion where it just flows. This is important because, again, it has to do with the interaction between you and your subject. If your posing technique is nothing more than an aggravation, an experience that is very awkward, and your subject just can't wait for it to be over, they'll look back at the photo session with a negative view. And a large part of it has to do with posing.

This is an area that we don't often talk about or emphasize, but it is an area that is crucial to productivity and success of the creation, your product. It's an area where you can standout without anybody knowing, because, well hey, we're talking about posing. Right? But if it's something that you are good at doing and you are making it a fun experience, and getting great results, people won't look back and go, "Oh, that guy really knows how to pose." They will just know they had a good time. And then they'll start talking positively about the experience. And you want to get every possible edge you can, including favourable word of mouth like that out there in the community.

USING LIGHT TO ITS BEST ADVANTAGE

Posing obviously works with light. When we're talking about posing, we're also really talking about light because the two interplay with one another. And when you get a sense of mastery over posing and lighting, you get to the point where you are able to produce really good results. Like I mentioned earlier, almost intuitively, in a very Zen-like fashion, where you can create great results, this is what you're after. I suppose, for lack of a better suggestion, we can all start with the traditional posing methods.

Now, when I'm talking about traditional posing methods, I'm talking about short lighting, broad lighting, feminine pose, and masculine pose. It's really that simple but, at the same time, a lot of us just don't get it. So I would suggest you get out there and practice, practice, and practice. Practice the use of doing a good, strong masculine pose, which works equally as well on men or women, and feminine poses, which typically will only work on women. And practice broad lighting versus short lighting.

Of course short lighting is nothing more than the shadow facing the camera side. That's my general quick and dirty description of short lighting. When you have broad lighting, the shadow is on the opposite side, and the side facing the camera is the broadest side or the side that is most lit. And generally speaking, as a rule of thumb, that kind of lighting is not ideal because it broadens up the face. Narrow lighting, or short lighting, really carves out the shadow's long edge of the face nicely, and the shadow side, being towards the camera, creates a nice effect so that it slims down the face, which works most of the time as a rule thumb.

Of course there are always exceptions to these and every other rule. But it is important to start here, and to learn how to pose with the traditional posing methods. But again, I'd like to remind you, practice. And if you've been doing the same posing for years and years, and years, maybe it's time to break out of the box and start experimenting and practicing something different. If you need an illustration or photo to see what it is I am trying to explain to you, then you are cheating yourself and looking for the easy way. There is no easy way. You must start with your own imagination. Think about what I am saying until it hurts. See it in your own mind's eye. It will do you a world of good.

GETTING THE BEST FROM YOUR SUBJECT

There are other posing techniques that involve correctional techniques – the proper alignment of eyes, nose, cheeks, bones and everything else within the human anatomy – to de-emphasize certain parts that aren't as desirable, and to emphasize certain parts that are desirable. Of course, what I'm talking about here is flattering the subject and making them look their best. Does this come easy? Of course not. It's challenging. It's probably the one area where very little time is spent on it, in any form of instructional workshop or academic setting. Unfortunately, it's the kind of thing that you have to learn on your own and have to master on your own. So, what better reason do you need than to get out there and start practicing, practicing, and practicing?

Learn how to pose. Learn how to understand the human anatomy, how people sit, how their shoulders and all the skeletal and muscular structure interplay and work together, and when there's tension or relaxation, and when there's slouching, or when there's good posture or bad posture. And whatever it may be, you must understand how all of this stuff works. And to make matters worse, once that's all said and done, you now have to understand how to create the best lighting situation. And to even make it yet worse some more, you'll have to make the whole thing seem effortless, so that your client has a very, very good time.

Posing is an art form, in my opinion. And it is not something that you just read up on and then go do. It is something that you have to get deep within yourself and a craft that you must develop a strong mastery over.

When you reach down and pick up your camera, and you're about to do a photographic session, you want your mind clear of academia . . . it's almost as if the more you think about it, the worse off you'll be and the worse your results will be. Your hands and your mind should know exactly what they need to do – either consciously or subconsciously, so that your conscious mind doesn't lose that connection between you and your subject. It's almost as if the more you think about it, the worse off you'll be, and the worse your results will be. So there's a technical side to posing, as well. But what we have to do is master that technical side so that we can soon forget it and move on to the subconscious side – creating a strong bond between them, which ultimately creates strong, well posed images.

So posing is structure, yet it is not. Posing is easy, yet it is one of the most difficult things you will ever learn. I like to refer to posing in reference to us being directors, just like Spielberg or any other successful movie director. A good director is somebody who is able to give good, solid direction, and everybody will do so eagerly and understand it with very little thought and/or process. When you have this kind of an effect on people and they respond enthusiastically, you know you've reached a good point where you are able to create some great poses. Mind you, if you're able to have really good rapport and your subject's having a very good time, but your pictures are turning out crappy, they will still look at the resulting images in a more favourable light. But there's still something missing, and there are issues that you need to look at.

When you're posing, there's another element that I've been avoiding talking about, and that is expression. Expression, again, works with the lighting and works with the pose. An expression is something that is decided upon within yourself, knowing exactly at the right time when to fire the shutter so that all of these elements come together. The same basic rules apply for posing, that I talked about, will apply equally as well for getting the best expression. But it is far more contingent on your ability to have a personality that resonates positively with people.

THE BIG MOMENT

One system that I've developed over the years is that I try to create a certain momentum during the photo shoot. That's why I was speaking with a certain amount of disdain toward the photographer who poses-stops-poses-stops-poses-stops, then takes the picture. When you are looking at getting the best expression, if you create a certain amount of momentum and you keep things rolling forward, you are automatically relaxing your subject. This is critical. It doesn't matter if the first bunch of pictures doesn't count and are not that great. What's important is to set the momentum. I often will do this, especially with clients who are very stiff or uptight. I'll just start with a very, very loose pose. And I'm not going to worry about it too much, because I know that further on into the photo session, I will enhance it more.

It's far more important just to get something going. I'll often have a family or a couple sit down in a particular spot that I think is going to be workable, and I will just ask them to sit wherever they want. And I'll just do some very minor adjustments. I'll maybe ask mom to come in a little closer to dad, and I'll ask little Johnnie maybe to sit down instead of stand up. And then I'll just get the camera pointed at them. And you can tell when people are nervous. They often say, "Where do we look? Where do we look? What do we do now?". I'll say, you know what, "Just sit and relax for a second. I'll let you know very, very soon. I've just got to go do a few technical things with my camera, and adjust my lens and lighting, before I actually take a picture of you guys." And instantly people think, "Oh, good," and, "So, he's not taking the picture right away." Once I get to the camera, often that's a lie. I will start taking a picture. I'll have everybody look at the camera and I'll say, "Ah, okay, that looks good." And I'll fire off a shot and say, "That looks great."

It's important to send feedback to your subject. And when I set this kind of pace, this kind of momentum, part of what I'm doing is, I'm allowing myself a chance to do just that – sending a message back to them. And it's a positive message that everything is working out. Oftentimes people are scared when a professional is taking their photograph. They're sitting there waiting to be photographed, and they think there's some specific behaviour or thing that they're supposed to do in order to make it a success. But truly, it's not.

They don't have to do anything other than just relax, be themselves, and be in a state of happiness and joy. The more you have that, the better those elements will show up in the picture. So it's important to start this pace, this momentum, so that we can get over those initial phases of insecurity and nervousness. And that's how I do it. So, again, I'll just have them sit there and I'll start shooting, almost instantly with very minor instructions on my part, but then I'll throw feedback right away. And I'll say, "Ah, that looked great guys. Let's take another one." I'll just keep firing away.

And if a pose doesn't work, move on. It's very, very important to not get stuck on it or force it. If it doesn't, don't let them see you sweat. Don't let your subject stress-out or get all tense, because they will take it personally, and they will think that they are doing something wrong. And they will get more tense as a result. It's okay if a pose doesn't work. Do you know what you're going to do next? I never do. I just go on to something else. I never go in with a preset destination in mind, as to what it is a particular grouping of people are going to pose like. Mind you, I do follow some fundamental rules.

For example, I look for composition. I look for, obviously, good light. And I look for such items as making the mom or the women look good, because if you don't make them look good, your photo session might be for nothing; and I want to make dad look like he's the boss, he's the man, he's in charge. Often many men have a little bit of a belly on them, so I find ways to disguise those things, typically by having the mom or the woman pose in front of that area, and having her pose very elegantly with a very feminine pose in mind. And oftentimes, if she's got a little bit of a mid-riff that is undesirable, if there's a little child in the picture, I will pose the little child to cover up that area.

ACCENTUATING THE POSITIVE

There are 101 different ways with which you can use posing techniques to disguise areas that you want to have disguised, and areas that you want to emphasize. But you have to look for these things in the beginning, and you have to be able to spot them instantly, without very little forethought or making a big fuss about it. Just very casually work these techniques into your pose. Corrective posing is a large part of this Zen-like and intuitive approach.

I just know, when I'm looking at a family, what I've got to do. I just know that anything is possible, but at the same time, I've got to make mom look good, I've got to make her look like a woman, and she has to look as slim as possible and as feminine as possible. I've got to make dad look like he's in charge, like he's proud to have his family with him, and he's the head of the family. I know that doesn't fly with a lot of people, but it's still something that is an important, psychological edge that you have to introduce into your posing. And the children will be used effectively so that you get a sense of closeness, and you can also effectively use the children to enhance the pose or to enhance the corrective techniques that you're using to take a better, more flattering image.

So when posing people, you need a good, strong sense of direction, and you have to have the kind of personality that entertains, and that people are attracted to and respond to positively. You must create a momentum, a forward motion, so that things keep rolling forward. If something doesn't work, you just move on. Next. And you're following all of the fundamentals at the same time – fundamentals we've talked about already.

KIDDIE CORNER

When photographing very young children, obviously a lot of the strategies that go into posing will not apply. A lot of the posing is spontaneous and very spur of the moment. I have found in my experience, and especially after photographing thousands and thousands of young children, that trying to control or maintain some order in posing is probably as futile as anything, and it will only frustrate you to no end, when working with very young children. I often talk to the parents before I photograph a young child and get the thought in their head that what the child will give me is what the child will give me, and that's what I'll photograph.

That's why I like photographs, oftentimes, with little children interacting, maybe playing ball or reading books or little girls picking up flowers, because these are things that they enjoy doing. Oftentimes even responding to a parent, or to a funny story or a puppet story. These are ways to get a child, hopefully, to sit for an instant and look in a certain direction, and laugh or smile, or interact in some way, shape or form. I've found the best way to pose a child is by setting the stage for this type of reaction, and making sure I am at the right place to capture it – quickly – because the moment is fleeting. And to flood the scene with a lot of nice soft light so I'm not trying to tweak the lighting. Or if I'm photographing outdoors, I have an idea of where I would like them and I manoeuvre towards that area. And if they give me five to ten seconds, pretty much, that's all I need to photograph a very young child. Older children of course can be bribed.

With children who are three years and older, I bribe them all with toys and treats that have been parent approved, and I make a deal with them. I talk with the child, and I say, "Look, you can have the toy and the treat, as soon as we're done." I don't tell them we're going to have a picture. And I remind the parents not to tell them it's about them having a picture taken, or looking at the camera or looking at the man. I tell them we're going to go, and I'm going to tell them a puppet story, or a story about a teddy bear or something of that nature, so that you're talking and discussing things in the mind of a young child – it is something they understand.

When they walk into a studio, they don't understand all these contraptions and all this equipment. And in their minds, they don't interpret it as a nice picture at the end. They just look at it as potentially a scary place, or an interesting place that they might want to run around and touch, and play with everything. Other than that, it means nothing to them. But they do understand puppets and Barney, and teddy bears, jelly beans, balloons and books, and things that only a child understands. So, use all these things and negotiate with the child.

WORKING WITH SENIORS

When I'm photographing older people, often they are very tense. I find that older people don't like having their picture taken. It's probably because they're old and they know it, and they don't like looking at themselves anymore. This is a reality. And I can easily reframe this whole process in their minds by talking about their children. So when I'm photographing an older couple, if they've been married 50 years, most of them have children. And so I get them talking about their families, and oftentimes there are grandchildren involved. And I just constantly, constantly, talk about children and their children. And if at any point and time there's nervousness, or a reaction where they say, "I hate having my picture taken," I will just tell them, "Look, I want to let you know something, and that is that this session is about your family. It's not for you, so much as it is for your family. Your family would love to have these pictures." It seems that when I say that, most people understand that, and it immediately puts them at ease.

THE LONG WALK DOWN THE AISLE

And I use a lot of these same tactics when I'm photographing a wedding. You know, a wedding obviously is people, so why would it be any different? The only thing with a wedding is there are many ages and there are sometimes issues with certain family members, and certain stresses that you wish were not there, but are there nevertheless. And above all, there's usually a very limited time constraint. Things have to happen fast. When I photograph a family, the way I pose is very, very relaxed. And this is a good thing. It seems that most people like that, unless they see something glaringly obvious in a pose, I'll change it. Otherwise, I'll just keep shooting it.

Most people when they're relaxed, and they're looking good, and they're in their best tuxedos and their best dresses, they just seem to be more attentive and they just seem to stand in a more positive way. And they're more automatically photogenic. They are not as inclined to run away from the camera. Weddings will make your job a lot easier in that respect, but by the same token, you're limited with time. When I photograph the groupings of a wedding, I do it very, very quickly. Families, immediate families, extended families, parents, parents of the bride and groom – all these groups get done very casually, and very, very quickly. Usually, within 20 minutes or less. And people appreciate that.

THE ULTIMATE POSE

As you can tell, there's more to posing than meets the eye. But ultimately it is an important factor to successfully getting a really good product. And it involves more than just that final image; it's the whole process and the interaction that goes on between you and your subjects. They are being posed, but they don't even know it. You're posing effectively so that you can get a great shot and so that you can have something that is worth selling, and that you can end up getting maximum return on. This is why learning to pose and the mastery of posing are so important. I wish I could say it in an easier to understand, better way, so that you can easily grasp it, but unfortunately there is no easier way. Posing is tough, but at the same time, it's a cinch. But, it is something that we must learn if we want to succeed.

CHAPTER 9

See the Light!

"There is nothing worse than a brilliant image of a fuzzy concept."

- Ansel Adams, 1902-1984
(Photographer/Author/Conservationist)

It seems kind of bizarre, don't you think, that we're not actually going to show you any photographs, and yet we're going to talk about lighting. Something that is so visual. Personally, I don't think it's important. I think in your own mind you should be able to understand what it is I'm trying to convey to you. It all starts deep inside you. And it all starts as an idea. Lighting is so essential, so important, and so integral to photography. The very word, photography, means light; painting with light. Lighting encompasses so many angles, so many dimensions of photography, that it's good to understand it, and all its complexities, and all of its simplicity.

Lighting is a real conundrum in that it is ridiculously simple, but at the same time it is more complex than anything. I personally have been studying light and trying to get a handle of it, all my life. And frankly, I'm probably never really going to get a full understanding of it. And that's okay. It keeps me going, keeps me young, and keeps me hungry. I would like to share with you what it is I do understand about lighting, and how I find it applies in the day-to-day working environment, and how we should and can become stronger and better photographers, as a result of understanding and applying lighting.

LIGHTING SHOULD NOT CALL ATTENTION TO ITSELF

First of all, lighting in and of itself should never be too obvious. If lighting is added to a photograph for the sake of adding more than what is required, then it becomes obvious that there is either too much light there, or an abundance of light is adding too many distractions from the main subject. So lighting often should be the simplest application, even if we end up using multidimensional lighting, and adding many different light sources, keeping in mind that simplicity is the ultimate goal.

Lighting should never detract, but it should pull out. It should draw out the very root of the subject. When you keep this in mind and you realize that this is its job, and you focus on the other important elements, such as composition and rapport and expression, and you coordinate it all with good lighting, a good handle on lighting, you really develop a strong sense of mastery – developing a strong sense of control over lighting and understanding lighting at its very depth. It's critical to becoming a very strong and a very capable master of photography.

Let's just talk about the nature of light, as well. The actual light that, in my opinion, is the most important light is the shadow. The shadow, or what is known as the 'fill light', is important because it carries the tones and shapes that are within the main light, or the main, general tones that define the actual subject itself. I'll talk a little bit more about tones in a second. But I want to start off with talking about shadows and how shadows are like a big, giant wave, and everything else is like surfers on top of a wave. You don't really see what's below the wave, but you know there's a lot there. So proper control and use of shadow is, in my opinion, very, very important, because it's what the foundation of a good photograph is.

When we talk about light, there are really three things that encompass lighting. There are three things that influence lighting. They are distance, source, and angle.

Distance is the distance with which the light is from the subject. The further away the light, the smaller it becomes; therefore, it becomes a sharper light source. And of course, the light intensity falls off as the distance increases. But that has more to do with affecting exposure. I'm really just talking now about the way lighting affects the subject. So distance, and how far or how close the light is to the subject, will affect the look of the light on that subject. Bring the light in closer, it's broader, therefore it is softer.

The shape or the origin of the light source will also affect the nature of light. Is it a reflector? A soft box? Is it a large, open sky, or is it a cloudy, overcast day, or is it a sharp directional sunlight? Obviously these are different light sources with different characteristics. These will affect the look of the light on the subject.

And finally, the third thing that affects the way light will work on the subject, is angle. The angle with which the light is coming at, and towards your subject, will strongly influence the way it looks. Is it coming from a sharp angle, is it coming from a flat angle, is it coming from behind, is it silhouetting? When you understand distance, light source and angle, and you start to apply these things into your photography, that, in my opinion, is the beginning of photographic mastery.

It took me years to really understand what it is I am now telling you. And the first time it was taught to me was when I was at a Dean Collins seminar many, many years ago – actually more than two decades ago. Dean Collins talked about these exact same fundamentals of good lighting. And it was such a mind-boggling experience that, wow, finally somebody explained the lighting to me the way it ought to be explained. But I didn't get it right away. It actually took me a good year or more to just start to understand. And then it took me many, many years really start to apply it. So, it's important to at least start somewhere and to start at the very basic fundamentals. And those are the fundamentals that Dean Collins was able to teach.

THE GOAL OF GOOD LIGHTING

Good lighting should come into a subject and should caress the subject, and bring out the shapes, the textures, and the forms that we want to bring out. We get to decide how we want to interpret these elements within a subject, and the way we use light to do this determines how much mastery we have over light. In a sense, we are making light work for us. This is not haphazard or gratuitous. We need to be aware of all things lighting, and make decisions based on what we see and want as our final outcome. And we use light to create the form, the shape, and the texture. And from the light, like I'd mentioned earlier, the shadow is the base with which we build upon.

There are two other elements of lighting that work on top of the shadow, and that is the main tone, which is the true tone, and then the highlight tone. So, you have shadow, main, and highlight, or what is commonly referred to as a specular light. Two of these three tones are false tones. The shadow tone is not the real tonality of a particular subject; the highlight tone neither.

Picture the sun shining off a rippling lake. Let's say the sun is coming in from a back angle. I'm sure you've seen that before. And you get those circles of confusion and those bright sparkly highlights. The water isn't really that tone; that's just the nature of specular highlights. The same is true with any portrait. When you have a specular highlight or when you have a shadow tone, you have false tones. The true tone is actually the main tone, and it is the true rendition of the important parts of the subject. Although, in and of itself, it is kind of boring, you work all three together, to create a stellar looking photograph.

It's kind of funny though when you really think about it, that there are only three tones, just like there are only three things that affect light – distance, source, and angle. You have shadow, main tone, and specular. You break it down in that respect, it's kind of ridiculously simple when you think about it. Isn't it? But it all boils down to the same concept – simplicity. Lighting is simple, and yet at the same time it is universally more complex than anything.

One term you often hear is directional lighting. I think that's about one of the most ridiculous things I've ever heard – directional. Come on. All light is directional. Some people like to use it as if it's some mysterious element or lighting. Maybe you need to reach a certain level of mastery in order to get this "directional lighting." Well, the fact is, all lighting is directional.

THE GOOD, THE BAD, AND THE UGLY

What is bad lighting? Bad lighting, well, is bad lighting. It's pretty obvious. All you have to do is look at a photograph and you can tell right away if it's bad lighting. Now bad lighting in and of itself doesn't mean that the lighting itself is bad, because light is light. No matter how you use it, it's how you bring it into play with the subject and with the three components that I talked about earlier – angle, direction, and the light source. But light in and of itself is light. I don't care if you're using a flashlight, strobe, sun, reflected light off a wall; it doesn't matter. What really matters is how you bring it into play and create form, shape and texture, or your ultimate, end result – shadow, true tone, and highlights – because bad lighting will reveal bad composition and bad photography, quicker than anything else. And bad lighting is nothing more than bad control, not mastery over lighting.

When I train anybody, or somebody assists me on any kind of a photo shoot, I always like to explain lighting. And one thing I often will tell my understudies is, find the light. Always find the light, especially when you're working outdoors and creating portraits outdoors. Finding the light is critical. Learning to see where your light source is and understand where it's coming from, and how it's working with your subject, is where you want to start. Look at your subject or where you're going to place your subject. Turn around, go to that area, turn around and face towards the camera and you will be able to see what your light source is. That will tell you a lot. Learn to see the light.

You know, it's important to learn to see the light because you want to be able to, in your mind's eye, predict how light is going to work. The more you can see it in your own mind, the more you can apply it in reality. It all starts in the visual interpretation and the mastery from experience, that you obtain with working with light. But in your own mind, your own head, your own creative imagination, if you can see how that end result will turn out, how that lighting situation is controlled by light source, angle, and direction, it will all come into play together in the final result.

THINK DIVERSIFICATION

I believe the more diversified you are in your talents and abilities, to explore and work with and master light, the more well rounded a photographer you become. And it also makes life a lot more exciting. Instead of getting into a rut or getting into a pattern of working with the same lighting over and over, and over again, which many photographers and photography studio owners end up doing, it's far more interesting and far more exciting to learn all the different types of lighting and different lighting scenarios, and not just stick with a certain, set pattern, and end up doing that for decades. It just makes things a lot more exciting. It makes a lot more creativity. It gives you a lot more diversity. And it makes your photography more stimulating.

Now we're not talking about going in and photographing a large family grouping and trying to get some real funky high fashion art looking light going. You know there's a time and place for lighting that has to be practical. Of course, when you're dealing with many, many portrait situations, the lighting's main purpose, obviously, is to create a very flattering looking portrait. It's important to realize that.

Most of the time, at least for me anyways, in the studio, I work with small soft boxes for smaller groupings and larger soft boxes or halo lights for larger groupings, and a proper amount of fill light either through a reflector or through a flash fill. And there's no secret here to getting this all done properly. It is just really a matter of knowing how to work your shadow and main light and specular highlights, all together. But again, it's good to work with some real creative lighting techniques, perhaps when we're working with a young couple or sometimes with children.

And many times on weddings, we want to get into some unique angles so that we can give some really outstanding and different variations, especially in today's day and age, when digital photography is really taking the mystery out of photography. The genie is now out of the bottle, so therefore we really have to work extra hard to be extra creative. So our work is not only excellent all the way through, but our work is really unique and stands out above and beyond what they are seeing, many times, again and again, from everybody and every second person who now has a good, decent, digital camera.

WRAP AROUND LIGHTING

What is it with this term, wrap around lighting? I hear it a lot of times at seminars or from photographers who are teaching. The last that I remember from physics class, from what little college I did attend, and from what I do understand and know for a fact, and that is that light travels in a straight line. It goes from point 'A' to point 'B' in about as straight a line as is possible. Now of course there are certain exceptions to that, way deep in the universe when light will get sucked into a black hole, but that's another argument for another time, and another day. But as we understand it on this planet, light travels in a pretty straight line. So, really, it's confusing when you hear things like wrap around lighting. And let's just call it what it really is: a big, broad, soft, light source. It's nothing more than that.

Light does not wrap around a particular subject. Or what's this other one I hear all the time that I spoke of earlier? – directional lighting. Same thing. Well, all light has direction. So don't confuse the issue by calling it directional lighting or wrap around lighting. Or the other whiz bang math formula that I hear all the time, and I don't know it exactly, but it has to do with light falling off to the square root of something, something, something, something. I can't really remember it, nor do I really care, but it's the kind of thing that you hear in seminars where it will really cause me to roll my eyes, and it also affect a good deal of many people who don't know any better in the audience who think that, 'Wow! This is it. This is the secret.' Whatever.

Light falls off rapidly. That's all you need to know. As you back up your main light, distance wise, it starts to drop off in power pretty darn fast. And there's this formula, whatever it is, again I don't remember, that people pull out of their hat, like it's a magic bunny and it sounds really cool. Listen, there is no secret. There is no special formula. There is no hidden agenda, nor is there any level of photography where you will be ordained and or sanctified with the special knowledge.

Light is very simple, yet at the same time, it is very complex. Light will give you unlimited creativity, but it is bound at the same time by very strict rules. There's nothing more to it. The thing that will help you is to try and understand how lighting works – and that experience will be your best friend – by training yourself to learn to see the light. It's a very, very good idea to have your photography critiqued by a qualified photographer. Have many people critique your work. And also look at other photographers' works and/or look in magazines and books all the time. And look at different lighting.

Look at the light; see it; see what the photographer did and how he or she created a mood or a certain effect, by having the light fall a certain way onto the subject. Most of the time a well-crafted portrait is not done haphazardly. It is not done by chance. Nothing is gratuitous. Everything is pretty much, for the most part, done with some planning, and the touch of a master's hand was at play in order to create certain desirable results.

IMPORTANCE OF IMPACT

A good rule of thumb is whether or not the image has impact. Impact is the number one criteria for a good portrait. Whether it's a portrait for sale or whether it's a portrait for print competition. Impact is the number one rule of thumb that'll help determine whether or not the judges will like it or whether or not your client will like it. If you have impact, look at the image and look at how light contributed to the impact of that image. Oftentimes it is the leading factor.

If an image is nice, but you're not sure whether or not it's really well done, and has a certain amount of impact, it's probably a good print, but because you have to second guess it, it's probably not that great. Or if you have an image and it's a one shot, one deal, one hit wonder, it's probably not going to be that valuable to you because it's important to be able to create effective and high impact photography over and over, and over again.

Consistency counts for a lot. You have to be able to regenerate results using all the skills of photography, including composition and exposure, all the technical sides and aspects to photography, all combined with the most dynamic aspect of all, lighting. So if you have to second-guess, probably it's not that great. Again, you have to be able to do it consistently over and over again.

THE CINEMATIC APPROACH

One of my favourite places for looking at light is in movies. You can always tell a movie that has been really well crafted with good cinematography, assuming it's got a good story as well, but you can tell that the lighting was done very, very effectively. Most of the time you don't notice it. It's just there bringing the story to life. But as a photographer, look for lighting, look at the speculars in the eyes, look at the direction of the lighting, and look at the way lighting is used. In many, many occasions it's used at very strong directions, used with proper fill light, but also notice how many times they use side lights or kicker lights to create and enhance the illusion of depth using the light.

Light is all around us. We might as well learn to study it, learn to analyze it, train our brains, and our eyes and our minds, to constantly be on the look out for new and creative ways. And always ask yourself the question, "What if? What if I tried this?" Why not? Just look at things a little bit differently and push the envelope using lighting if you really want to create images that are of high impact and unique in nature. But of course, keeping in mind that you must start from the very fundamentals, start from the very basics. Because, just like a good solid building, the foundation is where it all begins, for it to have longevity and to have impact.

CHAPTER 10

Composition

"Knowing how to sculpt vivid mental images from particles of thought is a very powerful thing. In reality, it's the basis of every form of art, including sculpture, photography, architecture, speech writing, advertising, poetry, website design and all the visual arts, including filmmaking."

- Roy H. Williams
(Marketing consultant and author
of the Wizard of Ads book trilogy)

W hen you look at the definition of composition, you realize that it is basically a very important fundamental of photography, just like lighting.

Let's talk a little bit about composition, even if we only dedicate a short chapter. I feel it's very important to revisit this topic. And it is the type of topic that is so fundamentally important and sound, and that is something that we, as photographers and creators of images, should always keep an eye on, and never, ever take for granted.

Composition is really nothing more than a creation and a gathering, and the assembly of all the different elements within a photograph. When you look at a photograph, and if you look at the background, for example, a family portrait may not have a lot of composition working for it, because perhaps the emotion and/or the fact that it is more of a documentary style of photograph or an editorial style of photograph, that may be more important than the artistic and compositional values.

When I create studio sessions, I find that this is more so the case. However, there are still some composition rules that I will talk about, such as triangles and shapes, and different heights, which are all pretty standard portrait guidelines that many of you may already know. But it's, again, very important to revisit and burn it into our subconscious mind, so that the more we master these elemental truths, the better, and more spontaneous and more creative, we can become, and the more masterful we can be, during an actual portrait session. I feel this is very important.

When we're doing outdoor photo shoots, you'll find that there's more room for creativity; and on weddings and families or children out on location, where there are different elements, such as foreground, background and middle ground, that composition will present itself as something that you can have a lot more fun with. That doesn't mean that all your portraits that you're shooting outside should be totally off the edge, and have a high level of composition at all times. There are times when shooting studio style shots work very well outdoors, as well. What I like to do is create a mix of the two, especially when I'm shooting outdoors stuff. Composition plays and has a very important role, especially outdoors.

TALKING FUNDAMENTALS

Let's talk a little bit about some of the composition fundamentals. Again, we're talking about ideas. I want you to get a visual on the things that I'm talking about. Imagine in a portrait in your mind a subject, whatever it is, imagine there's something that is closer to the camera – we'll call that foreground. And the middle ground would be the actual subject itself, and the background will be whatever the background is.

Where you place all these three elements – foreground, middle ground, and background – they are important compositional qualities inherent in any worthwhile photograph. And this is an important part of creating an image using composition effectively. It is obviously not the only thing, but it is an important truth. Foreground, middle ground, and background – this creates depth. This creates an interesting visual representation of the image. So you have to decide, as a photographer, where to place all these different elements within the photograph.

Other things will help enhance this experience, such as the direction with which the foreground, middle ground, and background all lead one to another. For example, you may have lines, either a picket fence or a trail, or the edge of a forest, that leads from the foreground to the background or partially thereof. You know what I mean? Now this line, will be far more interesting if it is placed creatively, not at a vertical or horizontal, but more dynamically, such as diagonally or as a curve. These are things that help increase and stimulate the composition within an image, by placing the lines, either very subtle ones or very obvious ones, in a very dynamic way, by placing them diagonally or through the effective use of curves, or what is commonly known in the industry as S-curves.

THE TRIANGULAR APPROACH

The placement of your subject is critical as well. If you look at most classic portraits, you'll notice that there's a lot of triangulation going on. What am I talking about? Triangles effectively use subjects to simulate the look of a triangle, either as a family grouping or even as a couple. And often, you can even have an individual look like the shape of a triangle depending on the pose.

The way you pose people or assemble people in the portrait, it is important that you resemble the shape of a triangle. Why a triangle? Triangles are very, very strong. Think of the Pyramids. There's probably not a stronger geometric shape with a larger base, which points up to the sky. It is very visually stimulating, and it emotes power. It is a shape that is much desired, especially in most portrait situations, whether in groupings, in families, or even when photographing couples. How you place your subject is critical. If you do a boring, stale job by having everything very symmetrical versus creating a very stimulating triangulation, and properly and effectively using foreground, background, and middle ground – when this all comes together, it works. Now add in some dynamic lighting and obviously good exposure, and all the other technical stuff that goes with creating a good photograph.

THE QUANDARY OF QUADRANTS

The placement within the subject is what is called quadrants. There are, as a rule of thumb, four quadrants – bottom right, bottom left, top left, and top right. And for the sake of argument, you could say there is the middle quadrant, smack dab in the middle. Most interesting looking compositions are not smack dab in the middle. However, if you notice that, occasionally, an image right in the middle works, that is good composition. But what you want to avoid is the instant you pick up the camera, you point it and put everybody smack dab in the middle. This is a very bad idea, and it is a sign of amateurism and lack of experience.

You can tell that somebody does not have control over composition by the way they photograph small groups – small groups at a wedding, small groups of people standing. There will be way too much space from the top of the head to the top of the portrait, because they place all the heads smack dab in the middle on an imaginary horizontal line. Boring. Dead boring. Don't do that. Try to use very creative composition, even if you're doing a group. Sometimes all it takes is a tilt of the camera. It's amazing what a simple 20-degree tilt either to the right or to the left, or even a stronger tilt, how it will all of a sudden take what might be an average, ordinary composition and turn it into, all of a sudden, a very, very dynamic and a very stimulating picture.

PUTTING IT TOGETHER

Again, all these things work together. In composition, obviously, you have foreground, middle ground, and background. You have S-curves and diagonal lines, and the placement of elements within your subject, which lead to the main subject and have direction and flow. And then, of course, there's the placement in quadrants. So, all these things come together. But here's the tricky part. You know, you really have to be able to do all of this very spontaneously, because composition, in many ways, is intuitive.

If you want to see this in action, all you have to do is give a camera to a 7-year-old child, and say, "Here. Go take some pictures of anything you want for the next 20 minutes." And let them roam around the yard or wherever. And then look at the images that will come back. Children are very intuitive at this age, and they will photograph things right from the gut. This is what we have to do, all the while doing and knowing that we have technical mastery. Gets kind of tricky, but it is the final and most critical aim that we have to shoot for. And it is one of the reasons why composition and mastery thereof is very, very important. And the reason why I'm dedicating this short chapter to it.

And of course, at the very end of it all, we've got our rules – rules of composition. And rules are meant to be broken. So, hey, why not? Sometimes you've got to take all of these rules, and you just have to throw them out the door and do something totally against the grain, because it just works, and there's no other reason why.

Follow the basics of composition. Look at the way you place your images. Study other images. It's very important to know that there are elements in your image that work together through the power of composition. And that everything in the image is strategically placed. Nothing is gratuitous. You don't just pick up a camera and point and shoot. You have to have a sense of mastery over composition, so that when you look at an image you can place it with powerful composition without thinking too much about it, but knowing that everything in the image is there for a reason. If something is not there for a reason, remove it or change the angle. Everything is there to enhance the story. When you look at an image later, and you find it's a little bit dull, look at these elements. Look at all the placements. Look at all the subject matter. Are there things that are distracting? Are there things that are not dynamic? Are there lines that are just not flowing in any particular direction?

Know what I mean? Everything has to have a purpose, as well as being put together in a very dynamic and creative way with the power of composition. It's very much the same way a chef or an oil painter puts together a creation – something they are creating. They are using these elements. And it's the fundamentals of photography. And we are no different just because we are able to pick up a camera and all of a sudden we're photographers. That doesn't mean we are masters. We have to develop this skill.

THE POINT AND SHOOT FACTOR

I've said it before, and I'll say it again. A great way to master, and help get much, much better at composition, is by getting a point and shoot camera, and bringing it with you everywhere you go. I always have mine. I have a little Canon A85, and for years now, and through thousands and thousands of experiences and images, I have been able to fine tune and help hone my photographic skills with the simple use of a small point and shoot camera. Not only that, it's a lot of fun. It's amazing the amount of images you can get. It's almost like when I was a teenager and taking pictures for the pure joy and pleasure of it. And a point and shoot camera is small and light and very portable, and it helps you to hone your skills so that you're always on top of things, like composition and lighting, and use of triangles and shapes, and direction and placement of your subject matter within the quadrants, and the use of leading lines and diagonals.

A point and shoot camera is often a "practice" tool. It helps us hone our skills and keep them sharp. Guitar players have small practice amplifiers, bagpipers practice on those small, whatever they are called (they are much quieter!), practice tools. Why shouldn't we?

Weddings "Yuck..."

L et's talk about weddings.

There have been a lot of changes going on in the industry, and a lot of those changes have affected the wedding photography business. First of all, let me mention some of the attitudes that prevail amongst many photographers. There seems to be somewhat of a disdain and a resistance to capitalize and grow one's wedding photography business. It's almost as if shooting weddings is some sort of an evil activity and/or necessary evil. I've heard many photographers say, "Man, the money's good, but I really just hate doing them." I don't understand this attitude. It totally baffles me.

First of all, I love photographing weddings. I get a lot of pleasure out of them. You've got such a powerful event where people come together, often from great distances; and they come together in a ceremony. It's kind of ironic, don't you think, that the statistics with the almost 50 per cent divorce rate doesn't seem to affect the deeper hope and meaning behind the wedding, the deeper and impactive meaning behind the ceremony and the ritual. It is something that we don't seem to want to give up. And it's universal and it has been around for many, many, many generations. It just seems to be the way it is. And we keep getting married. And we keep producing children and families, and all of that stuff that goes with it. Something happens to people when they decide to get together and form a union. On its own, it doesn't seem to matter much. Ritualize it, and all of a sudden you've got a very powerful event and, obviously, a big photographic opportunity. And industry.

Given this situation and given the background behind the importance of a wedding, it is an exciting event, in my opinion, to photograph. Visually, the opportunities are amazing. The emotions are almost endless in most cases. So there are many opportunities to photograph. And what better way to photograph weddings than to go straight after the heart and soul, straight after this story.

I first felt the inclination and the desire to change my photographic style around the mid '90s. I had been influenced, at that time, by Denis Reggie, who is renowned by many as a photojournalistic photographer. Back in the '80s I had been influenced by people such as Steven Rudd and many others like him, who are more traditional and more focused on the pose, the very grand style of wedding photography. I thought that this was a really great way to photograph weddings, but I knew that deep inside I had to evolve. And Denis Reggie's style led the way for me, because of his philosophy and approach to weddings. He held the clue to what is now my style of photography – what I call the freestyle wedding.

I like to break wedding photography styles into three categories. Essentially there are three ways with which we can photograph a wedding. There is the traditional posed method. And at the opposite extreme there is the photojournalism, like Denis Reggie, where 90 percent of the wedding is photographed with absolutely no posing; and only 10 percent, often less, is posed. There's an opportunity at some point during the day to do some quick groupings.

THE FREESTYLE LOOK

My style of wedding photography is what my associate, James Hodgins, has termed the freestyle approach. And it is a blend of very artistic and classical wedding photography styles, photojournalism and candid photography, as well as the more traditional pose. All these put together and in logical sequence, but reflected at the proper times and organized within a logical sequence, allow you to create what I believe is not only something that is a lot of fun to photograph, and allows you a lot of creativity, but it is something that allows the creation of a product that creates a lot of desire.

Other, non-visual, abstract elements are important factors that contribute to freestyle wedding photography – namely: the experience that the bride and groom, and everybody involved, have when you photograph them. First of all, freestyle allows for a lot of spontaneity. People like that, they respond to it. Especially when you have a leadership and confident attitude.

When I talk about the elements and the fundamentals behind freestyle wedding photography, a lot of it is very Zen-like. Although every wedding has to be very organized and planned in advance, when the actual day unfolds itself and the way you shoot it, has to be very spontaneous and almost seem effortless. For example, if you're photographing some formals, you have to get away from the mindset, and you have to get away from the idea, that I'm going to have everything planned. Instead, go in and allow for total spontaneity and be very personable. Allow your interaction to happen between you and the people, and work at the same time with the lights, with the poses, work fast, lots of momentum. And when you do this, the people feel very good about the actual experience itself. And this is a very important element to the freestyle wedding photography. It's not the only element, but it is one of the important dimensions that can't be forgotten.

I say this and make it sound easy, but the truth is – and for many photographers this is so – it is something that is not that easy to get. It takes practice. It takes the willingness to want to push the envelope and break away from our desire, and our wanting to be in control. You have to have mastery over the technical side of things in order to allow for the creative side to just flow in and evolve. You can get there, and you can become a very spontaneous and Zen-like freestyle wedding photographer if you push yourself, create that vision as to where it is you want to go, and be daring and bold, and push the envelope. It's a lot of fun. I have a lot of fun photographing weddings. And the more I do, the easier it gets.

When you're photographing a wedding, you'll notice that there are many other photographers or people with cameras, anyways. The genie is out of the bottle nowadays, especially with digital photography. It seems that every second guest at every wedding has a digital SLR camera and is capable of producing images that are on par or better than our own. That is all the more reason why we have to get away from the traditional style of very regimented and structured wedding photography. We have to be able to create a much more dynamic wedding product, and we must be able to create a much more dynamic experience. When you bring these together and you compare our images to everyone else's at the wedding who photographed with their cameras, it becomes obvious why you are of much greater value, and why your product is going to be placed on a higher level, and hopefully in a whole different universe and mindset.

TIME-SAVING TECHNIQUES

Another element, and this is important, is the idea that we spend so much time photographing the wedding and then we spend so much time working after the wedding. This, in my opinion, is an outdated, old school mentality. And a lot of photographers hang their hats on this excuse, where 'there's just too much work and the dollars per hour net income isn't worth it'. I say, this is a pile of nonsense. The fact is, all of my weddings are high profit exchanges where my cost of sale is a very small percentage of the final sale. And the actual hours involved in most of my weddings are on average five or six hours. How can I do this?

The solution is in the way I've positioned myself and created good products, with a lot of built-in desire. I've eliminated wedding albums from all my packages, and I've created them as "a la carte" items. This is an area that a lot of photographers seem to have a hard time letting go of. My wife who manages our studio, calls it a photographer's vanity. Call it that, call it ego, call it whatever you want. We seem to get caught up and pig-headed sometimes, and can't let go of some of these ideas. It seems to be more important to us, than it is to the bride and groom, that there be an album as part of the package. And of course, I mention albums because albums are such a heavy time element, and such a heavy cost element. It increases the amount of time we spend, and the amount of cost by putting together that product. They're very expensive and very time-consuming. Well, I've eliminated that equation by creating a product that is based on other things that are, in my opinion, far more desirable and far more important, as long as I educate my wedding clients and include it in my presentation. And I'll share that with you now.

In my opinion, the wedding album has been replaced by the slide show. I have been, since the beginning of digital, pushing and using slide shows because I am such a huge believer in them. I hear some photographers tell me really ridiculous things like, "Well, I use a Mac and I don't really have that many software options for creating slide shows." Come on. As if you would use that kind of excuse. My answer would be, 'get a PC'.

Do whatever it takes to be able to create this dynamic and desirable product. Don't get hung up on brand limitations and excuses that really have nothing to do with where it is you're trying to go. But the slide show, when combined with music – and by the way, I use very, very few transitions and effects in slide shows, because transitions and effects in the slide show take away from the images. The images are what it is you want to shine and tell the story. You don't want the transitions and effects to distract from that. When I first heard that, that made a lot of sense. And although I never used to use a lot of effects, I did use them and I brought them way down to a very minimal use in my slide shows. So, our core product is based on the photography. Not the album.

When a wedding client or a prospect comes into our studio, we really try to educate them and try to promote the idea that you can't compare apples to oranges here, because everybody else's apples or oranges are different. Our wedding photography is where their money is being invested. We try very hard to eliminate the whole comparison of product to product, and get their mindset away from comparing our product, our photography, our service to everyone else out there. And of course, we try and let our personality and our ability to create a relationship with them work its magic as well, because this is essential.

So when they come in, we show them samples from previous weddings. Often that's where they get it instantly. And I also use a lot of long copy, multi-page information and/or sales letters, and I inform the prospects to the absolute ninth degree as to how important it is that they understand what the freestyle wedding photography method entails. Most of the time, for me however, this is not really a major issue. Why? In my community I'm fairly established, so there is the benefit of being known. You should never take this for granted though. And I never do. There are still some prospects that need to be educated, and need to be brought up to date.

Many clients, when they come in, have one idea, expectation or price in their mind. Once I go through my presentation, my marketing sales pitch, and if it comes to them as a bit of a shock, that's okay. They'll leave, and often it will take them a few days in order for them to readjust their thinking. And I understand that. This is a process that happens quite often with wedding clients. They have to go home. And I kind of have this idea in my mind.

I can visualize them at home. The bride has a strong desire to want to hire me out. She's looking at the price and thinking it's more than they anticipated. Her fiancé, who is being very logical, would say, "No, this guy's too expensive." And there's this tension, so they have to discuss it. They have to resolve it – maybe something like the bride's father will enter the discussion and he'll see how his daughter really wants this; and maybe he'll say, "Well, I tell you what. I'll contribute 'x' amount of dollars." And that makes her fiancé happy, makes her happy, and it all works. Little things like that or other methods or solutions come to them. But we have to allow them to be in that position if they are indeed initially reluctant and/or have a different mindset, and expectation, as to what it is they thought the wedding packages and services that we offer were all about.

Education and informing our prospects is a large part of getting and achieving success in freestyle wedding photography. Once that is done, your relationship works wonderful magic. It seems that the more you charge, the higher the fee transaction, the more respect you will achieve. If you start marketing and selling, and competing with everybody else on price alone, you will notice a different shift in mood and attitude from your clients. But when you bring it to a higher level, when the transaction dollar amount is much higher, the respect level seems to increase dramatically. And this makes your job a lot easier. And this makes your bank account a lot better, as well. And that's a good thing.

When it comes to time involved, because we do slide shows and we focus on selling the photography as the core product, it takes a lot less time. The way I do it is, I sit after a wedding and I workflow each image. I go through each one in file browser in PhotoShop®, and I make a decision. I just open one image up at a time, then I make a snap decision – do I keep it or do I lose it? And you get good at this after a while. It's slow going at first, but now I'm able to workflow an entire wedding from say 1,200 images down to say 650 workable images. I can workflow these in about three to four hours. But you have to train yourself and you have to allow yourself time to get the experience up there, so that once you get there, it's like riding a bike. Really, it's a talent and skill that you never lose, you never forget, and you get quite good at it.

Once I open an image and decide I'm going to keep it, I instantly decide – does it go black and white, does it go colour, or am I going to do some burning in, or am I going to do any other soft focus effect or what not. And all of those applications are done in PhotoShop® actions. So my actions are the key to fast workflow. The average image takes less than ten seconds to workflow.

If you've ever seen me working a wedding, you'd see it's like watching one of those people who work their magic at the loom or when they create a weave. You know those contraptions where they're running yarn through, and they're creating a blanket, and their hands are going a mile a minute? That's me working on a wedding. And hey, I'm having a good time, too. This is very much the same experience that I had when I first fell in love with photography – that this is the darkroom.

This is when the image pops up and is developed for the first time. So when I look at my images that I created, I get a thrill each and every time, because I'm creating, and not only that, I'm taking the images and I'm bringing them up to a new level. This is a lot of fun. This is to me, what wedding photography, or actually photography in general, is all about. It is that instant when you see the image come up for the first time in the developing tray, or of course nowadays, on your computer monitor. It's a thrill that probably will never go away; at least I hope it won't. And I still enjoy it immensely, and I get a lot of satisfaction out of working the images and having a lot of fun, especially nowadays, with digital photography taking the images to a whole new level.

It's the same as when we used to have our darkroom and we used to do all of our own retouching in-house, except those methods were very, very slow, time consuming, very expensive, and very difficult and challenging at times. Well now, in nanoseconds, compared to the old days, we have literally a thousand times more options and creativity available. And it's really nothing more than the same fundamental idea that is a darkroom and retouching parts room, with all of the options, plus more, available to us. So, when I'm work flowing a wedding, I apply all these skills. And it's so exciting.

Some photographers seem to get caught up and end up going down different roads with this, and I don't know why. One of the roads is, they shoot RAW, and then they have to workflow all of their images down to JPEG, or they even go to TIFFs. And I have no idea why they do this. It makes no sense whatsoever. They're increasing their workflow substantially when they shoot in anything other than JPEG. You should be shooting in JPEG – after all you are a photographer – and knowing how to properly expose, knowing how to properly get white balance or at least managing white balance, is a part of the skill set that you should have. You should not be relying on fixing the problems that you're creating while you are shooting. You should be getting it right the first time. Besides, your sanity and the amount of time that you spend on the wedding are at stake. There's no other logical explanation for it.

THE RETOUCH

The other mistake that I sometimes encounter with photographers is that they end up retouching to the ninth degree, to get every file meticulous and perfect. This is nonsense. Although, my wedding files, when I deliver them as a slide show and as a proof, as proofs they look very, very nice. They are not the highest resolution possible. They are not retouched to the ninth degree. They are worked on, but they look good enough, and good enough is good enough. You don't want to spend too much time here, because in the long run the amount of work that you put into it to try and make it perfect won't really matter. And the reason is because each image really is not a stand-alone. Each image is a part of a series.

When you think about it, if I photograph and end up with 500 to 600 workable final proofs, they all work together from the first image to the last image as a series. It's almost like a movie. So I'm not going to go in and get each image 100 percent perfected. It makes no sense, because they don't really stand alone. Each image works as a part of a series of images that comes together to tell a story. Besides, if this were an issue, if in the marketplace I was hearing grumblings and complaints from my clients, I would perhaps change my view on it. But I don't have any complaints.

My clients love my wedding photography. And my prospects come in to me and for the most part, selling this style of photography is a cinch. It is not difficult to do at all. So I must be doing something right. But my point is to try and save you time and try and educate photographers to get out of this idea where they end up taking these distractions and going down different roads that really complicate their lives, and they end up hating shooting weddings, because it took them 60 hours to work a wedding after the wedding was over. And it's just not worth it anymore. If you're doing that, you're not shooting the freestyle way, and you're not delivering a product that is both beneficial to you, and beneficial to your client, and beneficial to your business.

Let's talk about the equipment for a minute. When I'm shooting a wedding, I use flash cards and I use a camera – my digital camera, the resolution is brought down to half resolution. I don't need all that memory for each and every image. And I also use three lenses. I could even, easily get away with two lenses, but I like the versatility of three. The lenses that I use are the 12-24mm Nikon F4, the 28-70mm 2.8, and the 70-200mm VR lens. I bring more flash cards than I need. And I make sure, the day before, to go through my equipment checklist, and I reformat all my flash cards. And I have them organized in a pouch that I watch with a very, very close eye. And I make sure it's within reach, and never risk losing it at all. That would be a tragedy.

TO FLASH OR NOT TO FLASH

I use a Nikon flash with my camera. But when I'm shooting during the day, I really don't use flashes that often. I try and work with natural light as much as I can. And I when I do use a flash, for the most part, I try and bounce it off a card or off a ceiling. Sometimes, I will get inspired to experiment and have fun with the creative use of multiple flash combined with the ambient light outdoors – time permitting You have to be able to assess each situation when you're in them and look at what is required to get the shot.

I can't stand those shots that are brightly lit by flash; and they are so obvious. I find that lighting so distracting and flat. When I shoot the reception, and by the way, my reception coverage lasts on average an hour, and that's not the way it's always been. I, for the last ten years, never even shot receptions, but have been shooting receptions more so in the last two years, because they've been more exciting and offer more opportunities.

When I do go to the reception, however, I bring multiple flashes with my Pocket Wizard®, and I want that multi-dimensional flash effect. I don't want my photography to look like everybody else's. You don't want to risk doing that. And that's where that one flash on camera look happens. If you only have one flash, at least drag the shutter and pull in a lot of ambient light so you can blend your flash and the ambient, and you can stand out above the rest. But if you can afford to get some Pocket Wizards® and a couple of spare flashes, go for it. My friend James shoots with used, cheap Vivitar flashes that he purchased on eBay. He sets them up with a Pocket Wizard® and gets amazing results. He did not spend a fortune on that system. And he gets incredible images like I've never seen before.

During the actual wedding day, the flash is predominantly used at the reception and at the church ceremony where the procession and recession happen. There may be other times when I might use a flash, but it's totally arbitrary and dependent on the situation and need. I work very hard to try and work with the natural ambient light that is in each and every scene. And this is where it could be a big challenge for a lot of photographers, because seeing the light is a skill set that you must develop, and you must develop the ability to relate and keep a very positive and a very forward momentum when you're photographing and directing.

You have to keep things going at a steady pace so that it's almost like you've created a wave and everybody is riding that wave with you. If you sit back and kind of say, "Okay, well what do you guys want to do now?" You're really giving up control, and you won't seem to be somebody who is in control, and somebody who knows what they're doing at a higher level. It's okay to ask that question, but as long as you don't lose that perception. You have to be seen as somebody who's like a Spielberg, a director. You're directing a movie, and you have to be in a positive and courteous, yet confident way, somebody who is able to lead the whole series of events to a forward and positive conclusion. This is important.

When you're applying this and you're also trying to look at the lighting, and you're trying to get some pretty cool and funky poses done, it can be a daunting task, especially if you're more analytical and left-brain. So I urge you to really push yourself to try and do things from a totally bizarre and different angle, and develop the ability to shoot images that are distinctive, and that reflect a style that is uniquely your own. I also never use a tripod when I'm photographing weddings. I will however, bring a reflector and sometimes creatively use it when I feel need to balance light back into my subjects. But I travel very light, lean and mean – three lenses, one camera. I have a camera back-up buddy that I typically keep in another camera bag that I don't lug around with me. It generally will sit in the car, or nearby, where in case of a mishap or whatever, I can go get it right away.

So, weddings don't suck. They're a lot of fun, and you can make a lot of money. How much money can you make at them? It depends on how you're willing to work. I'm generally happy with grossing about $80,000 a year. I don't like to photograph every single weekend. And generally 20 to 25 weddings is the amount that I like to photograph. $80,000 a year is my gross sales on average; it goes up some years, goes down some others. But my cost of sale is about $10,000. So, most of that is net profit, pre-taxes. And I'm happy with that.

That combined with my other portrait sales, and the fact that I'm not spending so many hours and days, and weeks, working my wedding images, makes for a good balance. And it allows me to be more creative and productive as a wedding and portrait photographer. Could I increase that amount? Absolutely. If I wanted to, I could supercharge my marketing. I could add many more ways in which I could increase the amount of weddings I photograph. I could even, if I wanted to, increase the amount of sales per wedding, but that all would involve more time and well, sometimes I just would rather take a holiday and go away with my family, because we need to have a balance in our lives and set our priorities straight.

So when you can photograph a large enough amount of weddings to make you happy and meet your goals, why not? Why not go for it? So, why not shoot the freestyle way where you have a product that is not only a lot of fun to shoot, but it's a product that is very desirable in the marketplace. It keeps your creative juices going. It keeps your bank account happy. And it keeps balance in your life.

CHAPTER 12

Photographing Babies and Children

"It's not who you are inside, but what you do that defines you."

- Childhood friend of Bruce Wayne
(Batman Begins)

I f you don't like kids or if the smell of a smelly diaper really turns your stomach, then skip this chapter. Go on to the next one.

But, if you would like to increase your profitability and tap into a lucrative market that is a lot of fun, a little bit taxing on your patience, but for the most part, an area that is relatively not that difficult to accomplish, then keep reading.

Babies are beautiful. There's nothing more exciting in a couple's life than when they first produce or create a new life. When you look at a wedding, it is my opinion that a wedding has a deep underlying subconscious meaning at a much, much deeper level. The union between two people holds a higher anticipation, a higher hope, and that hope is the creation of a new life. I think that that's why so many couples like to be photographed near water and in nature. Nature and water seem to be and tie in with this whole idea of a new life. When a baby comes along, it is a very hopeful time. It is a very exciting time. And it is a time that, for the most part, parents want to capture – especially the moms.

I started getting into shooting babies and children when my daughter was born. I always used to do a fair amount of them, but I really went after the market once my Danielle came into my life. And I've developed a whole new appreciation for what it was like to be a parent. This may or may not be important; I think it is to some degree a bonus when you are a parent and you begin to understand babies and children. If you're not a good parent, there's probably a chance you're not going to be good with children either. Like I always talk about in *Success and Marketing Principles*, everything starts with you. If you're good with kids, if you resonate with children and babies, you'll probably do very well. So you have to really look inwards. If you can't stand or don't think you're going to be any good with children, just skip this part altogether.

But I'm a big kid at heart. And I really believe that children are very, very creative and that they are very spontaneous for obvious reasons. When I'm photographing children, I try very hard to create a bond with them. And this bond is harder to do, if the child is younger. I'll try and touch on this a little bit more and explain what it is and how it applies, in a day-to-day shooting environment.

IMPORTANCE OF COMMUNICATING WITH PARENTS

When I have an 18-month-old come in the studio, I know I am in for a challenge – it's the most challenging and difficult age. The first thing I always do, is I discuss with the parent what my plans are. And that is basically, that there are no plans. So, I remove many expectations from the parents, so that they don't think that their child has to behave a certain way. Sometimes parents have an idea in their mind as to how things should go, either because they think the child has to respond to me in a positive way or they just have a certain behaviour discipline mindset that should be applied to their children. I try and remove this entirely. And so I always work through the parent or adults that enter into the studio when I first photograph a child.

The first thing I do is I sit down, and I ask the parent to sit down. And I tell them right way, I say, "Look, what I'd like you to do is just talk to me, because your little guy or little girl is checking me and this place out. They need to know that this is a safe place. So I want you to just talk to me, because they're looking at me and seeing that I'm your friend. And I want them to get comfortable and eventually create some sort of a bond with them. And you, the parent, cannot help with that process. But, the thing that you can do is to let it happen and get your mind off your baby." Now most parents understand this, but they still resort to controlling behaviours. So I have to typically wait it out. And

I anticipate this, and I anticipate the behaviour of an 18-month-old. So it doesn't surprise me when things go straight to 'hell in a hand basket' and there's total chaos that results. I expect it. If it doesn't happen, it's a bonus.

I work through the adults, and it's all psychology. I understand children. They do need to bond with me at their pace. And their natural curiosity, of which we all know they are loaded with, is the key. So what I will tell the parent is, "I'm going to place an object in the middle of my studio. I don't want you to point it out. I don't want you to point out any of my toys. The child can see very much on their own, and they can hear. They can hear me, they can hear my squeaky duck, and everything that they are perceiving, happens on their own. The more that the adult tries to intervene, it seems that Murphy's Law kicks in. And that's when oppositional bonding happens, and the child says, "No." So, again, the whole key is working through the adults.

BEST PROPS

The one thing that I like to work with is a chair, a very simple chair, or a squeaky toy. I don't know exactly how each session is going to unfold, but I know in my mind that eventually something is going to happen; I just don't know what it is that I'm going to do. I follow these strategies that I've discussed so far, and I wing it. This could be very difficult for a lot of photographers. You have to allow that process to happen so that when you go into a studio session with a child, you have to create the free flow attitude and lose any expectations. Because if you have expectations, and they are not met, you'll just end up with frustration. And that's not a good thing.

STAGE DIRECTIONS

I often will do one of two things for the first part of my sessions with young children, around two years of age. I ask the parent to pick them up like they normally would, and I ask them to stand beside the spot where I'm going to photograph them. And I remind them, "Don't say anything. And when you put the child down, don't walk away. Just stand there." Because if they walk away, it gives the child something to look at. But I want the child to look at me. And I will start squeaking my little toy and get the child's curiosity. This works about half the time. And when it works, I will get about five to ten seconds, and sometimes I'll crack a smile. So I use a squeaky toy that they haven't seen yet. And they just stand there and they look amazed. And if I go peek-a-boo and do whatever silly noises I have to behind my camera, I might be able to crack a smile.

Sometimes they'll run towards me, and I'll just ever so gently remind the parent, "Okay. Good. Pick him up again." And just repeat this process. This works a few times, but then it wears out. After that I often will simply take a quick one or two minute break just to let the child check the place out some more. And I'll remind the parent, "Don't point this out," and I'll grab a small chair and I'll place it in the middle of the studio. Nine out of ten times, the child will see the chair and go on there on their own. If the parent says, "Oh, look. It's a chair," it seems that, again, Murphy's Law, the child stops and says, "Ahhh, no." You want me to, therefore I won't. So as you can see, I am using a lot of reverse psychology, and it works for the most part.

LETTING PERSONALITY SHINE

I should mention, too, that I've told the parent, either on the phone and reminded them again in the lobby, that I don't know what poses and/or expressions I'm going to be able to get; and that a lot of it is based on what the child gives me. It's a lot of spontaneity. That's actually a cool thing. And it's actually a saleable angle when photographing children. Most parents seem to like that. The old school way is very posed, very traditional. The new way is to let the child's personality shine through. Let their uniqueness shine through and capture it with some dynamic images.

Sometimes I will photograph very close, tight shots of their face, and I'll tell the parent I will be doing that. And the cropping will be very unusual. That way I am pre-emptively telling them and managing their expectations. So when they look at these weird and unusual crops, they know, 'Oh well, that's Rob's editorial style that he talked about.' Parents often seem to get into this whole smile business, that the child has to smile. And it's okay to get some smiles, but as I remind the adults and parents, most of the favourite poses seem to be the poses that are serious. And I will point out the many samples in my studio, and I'll say, "Look. Look at all the wonderful poses here. The parents love these poses. Did you notice a common theme? The vast majority of them are serious."

The child has an expression. It's the expression. And it often comes through in the eyes. That works the best in most of these portrait situations. But again, I'll try and get some smiles and really try and get the uniqueness and capture that distinctive, expressive quality that each and every child has.

PRODUCTS AND PACKAGES

Photographing children and babies gives you many opportunities for selling some very dynamic packages and memberships. I got my photography business going by creating the Kreative Kids Club, which was an 8x8, leather album, which cost me at that time $22, and it was very nice and unique. It was very funky. Part of that membership is a five-year membership, and it included a portrait session every six months for five years, and a 5x7 from each session. And of course we promoted the fact that we had a jelly bean machine and we had free toys for the children, and we had these really cool photographic styles that we did. Now when people joined the club, they would also get a small discount on reprints in unit.

Most photographers are aghast when I tell them about the Kreative Kids Klub. They are stuck in the dollars per session mentality. The truth is the Kreative Kids Klub is a membership, like Costco®. It not only gives clients an exclusive sense of belonging to an exclusive membership, but it is really nothing more than a lead generation tool. It gets people in the door.

Now our average sale for children isn't as high as family portraits, and the system that we use, although it can be improved, allows us for minimum time and work. And I'm okay with that. I don't want to go into each and every portrait situation and have to sell a 30-inch portrait. That is not my objective. I don't care for that. I'm looking at the big picture here. And the fact is I'm having a lot of fun photographing a lot of these children and families. And by the way, many of them will lead into bigger opportunities. You get your name known and deeply entrenched in the community through your child and baby portraiture.

Who knows where that mom works? She could be working at a place that might eventually need photography for some other purpose. Or they may, at some point and time, be getting a family portrait, which happens very, very often. So it leads to bigger and better things. But that doesn't mean you should give away the farm and sell your stuff dirt cheap. You should still command a respectable profit from your work and not undercut yourself. But we do sell our children re-prints and packages at a reduced price. We want them to feel that, yes, this is a special category – we are a member of the Kreative Kids Club.

Memberships work. If you don't believe me, just look at Costco® and all the other places that use memberships as a major marketing tool. Even Chapters and other bookstores use memberships. This is a wonderful way that creates a sense of belonging, a sense of belonging to a special group, and they have special privileges. And it gives you an opportunity, as well, to send them other communication, either through e-mail or direct mail, of which newsletters are my favourite form of communication. So, when you do this, you create a relationship initially through the membership, and you enhance it through future communications. You really create a strong relationship and a bond with your clients.

The relationship with your client is a very important asset. And if you are of the mindset that you need to create a certain amount of dollars per hour, and you have to sell wall portraits all the time, you're probably just going to end up banging your head against the wall. When you create memberships and you sell packages, you have to understand, it's the overall picture that you want to achieve. And of course, lifestyle and balance plays in that too.

Not only can you use memberships to promote and market child and baby photography very effectively, but you can also create similar memberships, such as the popular Baby's First Year Wall Panel. We've been successfully doing that, and running a campaign based on a two-page sales letter since 1997, and have literally photographed thousands of babies as a result, with a lot of success and a good profit. We've also created what's called a Siblings Package, which we offer to some clients who have siblings, and we only send these letters out to those that we decide we want to keep as clients. There's also the Toddler Panel, which is similar to the Baby's First Year Wall Panel. And it is a logical progression from the Baby's First Year Wall Panel and is available for the children after their first years' photographs. And you can keep photographing them for the next two years, or actually the next year, as they get into the toddler phase of life.

So as you can see, there are many options and many creative ways with which to package and bundle neat membership deals that are very attractive. And when you do this, you create a message that is powerful. You create a message that is easy to describe. And you can create offers. The heart and soul of marketing is creating a very innovative and a desirable offer. Of course, based on a good solid product. You must have a good solid product, good photographs to start with, and any targeted group of people, which in this case is very easy to define.

That's another reason why marketing to this group is for the most part a lot easier to tackle compared to many other markets, because they are so easy to define, and they are so obvious. But of course, you have to be willing to photograph children, and you have to have the desire and the talent to work with children. Other products too are: Creative Composites, Creative Multi-Image Panels, and Mini Albums, and bracelets with pictures, and all of these other ideas that are either used as main products or premium items that could be added to any package or bundle.

Think of McDonald's®. You know you go to McDonald's® and pretty much almost any drive-through restaurant nowadays, and they have specials. They have deals. These are nothing more than package deals. And the reason they do that is, because they work. Just because it's a fast-food restaurant doesn't mean we can't use it. And a lot of the innovative and creative marketing packages that are made for baby and children portraiture are very much along the same lines as this style of marketing. So we can borrow and we can use a lot of these same ideas. Why not? It works for them. Why can't it work for us?

And of course, there's the super size up-sale, which we should still be using as well. In our studio we have three versions of the Baby's First Year Wall Panel. There's the gold, the platinum, and the platinum plus. And the gold is very desirable, but the platinum plus is even more desirable, and it increases our profit margin substantially. So, the people who come in to get the gold, a certain percentage of them, probably about 30 or 40 percent, will upgrade to the platinum. Why? Because it's there, and it's an obvious progression to them. But if you don't do it, if you don't make it available, you're not going to sell it.

DISPLAYING YOUR PRODUCT

When you get a good selection of samples of baby and children photography, you have some excellent tools with which to use on your website or any literature or displays. Babies and young children are so visually impactive, and they are such a draw for all of these purposes. If you do a display in a mall, be sure to load it with a lot of baby and children portraits. It'll just draw a lot of your target into your booth, especially women who are the main decision makers. Those are the people you want to be drawn into your booth and into your studios.

I have successfully marketed through affiliations in my town, and through local stores over the years. I would do photo shoots at stores where they sold all kinds of clothing, and items related to babies and young children. And I also was able to put displays up. Other stores included high-end children's stores where for years and years, and years, I managed to successfully have a wonderful display where everybody saw it. I also held draws where I collected names, and these names went into my database at these stores. So there are many dimensions to going after this market. And you can't really go after one and expect it to really build your whole business. You have to be able to successfully list all the potential areas and avenues with which you can market to this area, and go after each and every one of them. And make sure to do so with a complete and follow-through methodology.

SLIDE SHOWS – THE WAY TO GO

Just like with my weddings, but to a lesser degree, we use slide show DVDs for our baby pictures. Our platinum package for the Baby's First Year Wall Panel includes a series of images from each photo session, typically at newborn, 4, 8 and 12 months, or 3, 6, 9 and 12 months. And we collect about 20 to 30 images from each shoot and end up with a total of about 100 or so images that we create a, roughly, seven minute DVD show with titles and a customized DVD case using the baby's images. It doesn't take very long to create these products. And they are very, very desirable. Many moms are very deeply touched by them. And they can be used to promote these packages, and to promote to future prospects. But you have to be able to create them in order to sell them.

Put them in your packages. Make samples available. Show your prospects; show them how dynamic they are. Explain to them. Use them as up-sales or premium bonus items. But they are not like weddings in that they replace the wedding album. With baby pictures, the DVD slide show is just another product. The baby sessions will still require things like small albums and reprints and what not, including all the other reprint specials, such as greeting cards and what have you.

A WILD WORLD

If you've got what it takes to tackle the wild and wacky world of baby and child portraiture, you will tap into a fairly stable and constantly regenerating market. And you can make some money and grow your studio, as well. It can also springboard you into other avenues, such as anniversary portraits, family portraits, and whatever else may come along. Always remember though, to never push children. Work the psychology through the adults and parents.

Be very patient. Know that you will get results. Know that you don't have to know how they are going to come about. Use very dramatic lighting that stands out from anything else they've seen or from the department stores' style of photography. You must get good at anticipating where the child will be in order to be lined up properly with the lights and hopefully having their bodies and heads turned and arranged in a certain fashion that they are lined up properly, so that all these elements work together, and you get good lighting and a good angle. It's a little bit tricky. It takes some time, but it gets easy like anything else.

When I photograph older children, it becomes much, much easier. But I still apply the same strategy. I work with the parent and I tell them, "Look, let me talk to the child. When I ask the child a question, don't answer for them." The parent almost always will answer for the child, and this breaks the union. This breaks the bond that I'm trying to create as I try to become a buddy with this child. Typically, I'll ask very simple questions. If they come in as siblings, I'll look at them and I'll say, "Hmmm. I wonder who the oldest is?" And if I didn't prep the mom, the mom will say whoever the oldest is. And so I don't want the mom to talk. I want to start an interaction with the child.

So the oldest, who's proud of the fact that they're the oldest, will usually swell up their chest and say, "I am." And I'll say, "Cool. So how old are you?" And if they're a little younger, they may not know that in the numerical sense. So I'll ask, "Show me how many fingers old you are." And then if they show me, say three fingers, I will look at them and point to each one and I'll count and gently touch them on the tip of the finger – one, two, . . . See what I'm doing here, again, it's all psychology. I'm creating not only a bond and an interaction, but I'm seeing if the child will let me touch them. I'm kind of doing it in a sneaky way, but still it achieves a bond in a much quicker way because we're talking about their age – something that they are very intimate with. And as I count, as a joke, I'll often stumble at the last number, and I'll go, "Two, hmmm, two. What's after two? I can't remember." And the child will blurt out, "Three!" And I'll say, "Alright. I forgot." Anyways, it's fun and it creates kind of a silliness that children so often can relate to. So that's a great way to bond with a child.

Another way is to bribe them with toys. I have a treasure chest in my studio, and I use it effectively. I ask the child, "Do you know what you're doing here?" And they'll sometimes know or not know. And I'll say, "Well, we're going to go over there and I have a camera and I'm going to tell you a story with the puppet. And we have Barney® here. And we have a treasure chest full of toys and you get to pick a toy out when we're all done."

See what I've done is, I've related the whole experience in their mind. And I mentioned camera one time or taking pictures one time. But it's mostly about puppet stories, and it's mostly about having toys and having fun and telling me how old they are. Children don't relate objectively to the whole idea of having a portrait session. So, the parent, who thinks that the child does, needs to be deprogrammed, and the parent can be involved in this process. So what I do then, is I show them the treasure chest full of toys, and I give them a quick peek, and I say, "Oops. I'm going to put it right here and as soon as we're done, you get to choose any toy you want. Is that a deal?" And they'll always shake their head up and down with a big, bright-eyed look and say, "Yeah." So I'll say, "Give me five." And then they give me five, and they allow me to bond that much closer to them.

Now if there is a younger child and an older child, the older child is the key to getting the younger child, especially if the younger child is about two years old. So, I will almost totally ignore the younger child and work my strategy through the older child. The younger child will simply follow, with no need for instruction whatsoever. Whatever I get the five-year-old or four-year-old to do, the two-year-old will simply follow along. They like to play along. It's like a game to them. And it makes sense. They're with their older brother or sister, and they're having fun. They're playing. This is an activity that they're used to – playing. And so, I may not have all the time in the world to get this done, but certainly enough time to get all the portraits done. So you have to be precise, and you have to expedite your opportunity to photograph when you're working with very young children.

CHAPTER 13

The Whole Family

"You can't depend on your eyes when your imagination is out of focus."

- Mark Twain, 1835-1910
(American humorist, satirist, writer, and lecturer)

Families can be fun, yet they can be very tricky. I want to talk to you about how I pose and work with families and how I market to them.

You can get a lot of family business, and make a lot of money at them, just by being very well known in your community and having business come to you automatically. Or you can be very aggressive – and you should be, especially if you're starting out – and go after families and family sessions by using some very direct, response related, and aggressive marketing strategies. Oftentimes, to begin getting your family business going means that you have to knock on people's doors, literally speaking, and make offers and pitches so that they come on board. If you're starting out, this is okay; and it's something that needs to be done. I did this for years.

Free gift certificates for free shoots are one method. You can have a free draw at a display in a mall and collect names for a, say, 20x24 framed portrait as a first prize draw, and send everybody else a letter that says they won an 8x10 in a second prize draw. You may think this a little bit sneaky and a little mischievous, but it works. It's a great way to get the phone ringing. Now, you will find a higher maintenance crowd when you offer things that are at that level, meaning that people have different expectations when something is free. So you need to manage them. You need to manage the process. And you need to have a solid sales presentation and systematic approach. But you will get the business going.

Another way to get business is to go after any weddings you're photographing and offer a free session for the bride's family, and a free session for the groom's family. You could do affiliations through clubs and organizations that you belong to, and send out a fund-raiser. Fund-raisers are amazing as far as getting respectable clients in the door. If you do a fund-raiser for an auction, a live auction is preferred because a live auction usually has the higher priced items. You can donate a framed print at a higher value, and try and target the rest of the crowd afterwards. Send them all a sales letter.

If you have a silent auction, you should ask to get the list of those names and addresses of anybody who puts their name down for the auction so you can contact them, and phone them, and send them letters. Because obviously they were interested in that particular item even if they didn't win the bid. And if you are smart about that, at any auction, you could and should mail to everybody who is there as long, as you have permission from the organizers of the auction.

OTHER INNOVATIVE OPTIONS

There are so many ways to get family business going. You can go through schools. You can go through banks and stores. You can have media driven specials for seasonal sensitive opportunities. And the most popular of course is Christmas time. Photograph in the fall and create a package with some desirable bonus items such as Christmas cards. This is effective if you're well known in the area, so that if you do use media, such as radio and/or newspaper, people recognize you. If you're not known yet, you have to make in-roads to become known. And I know of no better way than to do displays, and to use direct response mailers.

I've used postcards as well. Postcards are amazing. Although some marketers frown upon them, I think they work very well. Why? Because if you use a good postcard, with high quality stock, and they're so easy and cheap to produce nowadays, the first thing that the recipient at the home sees, when they go through their mail, is all the beautiful sample images displayed in your postcard. Beautiful sample images, and an effective headline, that should grab their attention. And you better have some good images to impress upon them what it is that you can offer them. So, on one side will be all of these images, and hopefully a good variety thereof. And on the other side, where the address is, you put a couple of headlines and you make a pitch for them to call you on an offer. That's one way to use postcards.

Anywhere where there are families, there is a family portrait business. It's all around you. Look at your neighbourhood. Look at your organizations. Look at the stores or a family shop. Look at the clubs and organizations they belong to. There are so many ways with which to create a family-based portraiture business. If you have people, you have families; you have business. There is no excuse not to tap into and grow this market easily, with a little bit of effort and a little bit of persistence on your part.

AN ON-GOING LOVE AFFAIR

I love photographing families. Families, to me, are very exciting. I don't know what it is. I just find them very special, especially younger families – when the children are between the age of five and 15. When they're much younger, there's that whole we're starting out in life kind of aura. When they're older, the kids are starting to leave home, and there's a different energy. Of course, when you're photographing families that have married children and you have three generations now, it's taking on a whole new aura, and it's more of a legacy than anything else. And these are potentially very lucrative portraits as well.

The reason I like families between the ages of five and 15 is because the kids are very easy to work with. They're not into their own independence yet, and they're still very much all bonded together. There's no major conflict and/or political family issues that are at play. It is just a joyful time. You can get a lot more variety then, and you can have a lot more opportunity to create some images that are visually very stunning.

THE GOLDEN RULE FOR FAMILY SHOTS

When I'm photographing a family I try and follow this basic rule – make the man look like he's in charge; make the mom look good. So I pose accordingly. I use triangulation a lot. Or I'll try some of those silly, fun poses that I've become known for. Heck, I'll do them both, whatever, to give them more variety to choose from. Following the more formal type posing, I try and follow composition rules where the basic family shape is in triangulation form. And dad would be at the highest point for the most part to make him look like he's in charge.

The mom must be sitting in somewhat of an elegant, flattering angle. But you can use younger children if you need to hide tummies or hips, or certain parts that you want to de-emphasize. I also try and get some walking shots if we're photographing outside. Just get a family holding hands, if they're that close, and walking away from the camera or to the camera, or scenes near the water, or whatever else is happening in that environment.

Sometimes you have to go with the flow of families and just kind of look at the relationship. Look for little, subtle clues. See what's going on. See what kind of an energy or spark, or if anything is going on between the members of the family. See if there's a unique bond between a certain parent and one of the children – mother, son or father, daughter – and work with that. Work with that flow. Just let it happen.

We try to consult with all our families as well, because oftentimes when the moms call, it's a very important thing for them to have a family portrait and they've often put a lot of thought into it. And it is something that they are willing to invest more money in, to use properly in their home as décor. So you want to make sure that you achieve some very desirable results, so that you can meet these expectations.

Now if you're starting out and you're doing a lot of promotions where you're getting more volume through and people are of a different mindset, you have to control and manage this much more. You have to be able to make the consultation a big deal. You have to suggest it. Oftentimes when you're established, families will call you and they'll just automatically fall into the proper stages and phases of getting a consultation done and preparing properly for the portrait. This is not so much the case when you're photographing or when you're getting families, because you're working a higher volume marketing strategy, such as free prizes or gift certificates. But it's easily done, nevertheless.

It's just that you have to educate, and get together to start to create a bond, again so that in the mind's eye of your subject and especially the mom, it's an important event. You have to, somehow, instil this value that it's very important and that the results that you're trying to achieve are very important to you, and that you achieve the very best. When you start there and you get it straight in their minds, then you lead to bigger and better, potentially more profitable, sales. And it makes the selling process later much easier. It won't work for everyone when you are dealing with the higher volume sessions, but worth the effort.

MARKETING TO FAMILIES

As far as selling is concerned, like I mentioned, when you are established and people call you as their choice of photography studio, selling for the most part is a lot easier. Their expectations and anticipation are much more easily managed, because they kind of know who you are through your reputation. But if they don't know you from Adam, you can, and have to, manage those expectations so that when the selling process begins after the session is done, one event leads progressively into the other.

If you avoid this, you will notice a very high failure rate in your sales process, and you will experience a lot of frustration. So when you begin to adjust the thinking of your potential clients and manage their expectations all the way through, by the time the selling process happens, they're ready, and they're open for it. Don't wait until the last minute to make this happen. The selling process starts from the first contact. It starts right away.

When I photograph a family I always photograph the parents alone, the children alone, and the children individually. It's just something I do. It increases variety and increases sales. Sometimes they don't even expect that to happen, or it might even intimidate them. But I don't care. I just do it anyways. I just automatically act as if it's routine. I'll say, "Okay," and I'll ask the children to move out and leave the parents there. And I'll come in and start shooting the picture of the mom and dad. I don't even give them a chance to reflect upon it.

By the time it's happening and over with, it's too late. But they usually are excited by it by that time anyways. And it's the same with the kids. I'll automatically say to mom and dad, "Okay, can you guys just jump out for a minute?" And then I'll start photographing the kids alone. Sometimes I get the kids to do some really fun and goofy things, too. And then I'll come in and photograph each child individually. I don't dwell on these, and spend hours, and hours photographing these poses. I try and go very spontaneously so that the energy in the family shoot is very high and very exciting; so that by the time it's over they can't wait to see the images. This is part of the sales process, like I just mentioned earlier. This is part of getting them ready and managing their expectations, so that by the time they do see the actual proofs, their anticipation level and their willingness to purchase more, is at an all-time high, unless of course you didn't do a good job and the product is not too desirable. But we'll assume for the most part that you did achieve good, saleable, desirable, flattering, and decorative images.

FAMILIES AND WEDDINGS

I might as well talk for a minute about doing families at weddings. Typically at a wedding, I'll do families, but I don't dwell upon it. And I do them very, very fast. It's not a really big deal, nor do I believe it is a big profit center. I largely want to keep it, most of the time, open for doing all the other photographs, but I do realize that family, on a wedding day, is very important. So I will photograph the extended family and the immediate family. And if, say for example, the bride's sisters want the picture with her husband and their three kids, I'll photograph that as well. And most of the time these things have been brought up earlier anyways, and approved by the bride and groom. I'll spend less than forty seconds or so photographing each and every one of these, so that we don't spend hours, wasting all our time, and lose the opportunity of photographing those precious wedding photographs.

Also when I'm photographing families at weddings, I like using my long 80-200mm telephoto zoom lens. I'll get way back so that I can shoot from waist up, typically open shade if I'm outside. And that way when I'm photographing them, I'm so far back it intimidates anybody else from getting in front of me and photographing, and stealing my pose. Not only that, but the main reason is that because I'm shooting with a telephoto lens, and I'm shooting at almost wide open, I end up with a very unique look. If anybody does happen to take a shot from the same angle I'm at with their point and shoot cameras, they probably will have the wrong lens or something that is too wide, and they'll end up having a totally different look than mine. And their images will look, well what can I say – amateurish. Mine will have a very nice, three-dimensional quality to it, very unique and only achievable using the right lenses and equipment.

I also photograph families as a part of the wedding, before the wedding. I don't do this as much now, but I used to offer the bride's family and the groom's family a free session and an 8x10 designer portrait. And my reason for this was so that I could get to meet the family before the wedding, and the family could meet me. But really, what I was trying to do is get more sales. I don't do this as much, but it is definitely worth considering. When you photograph the families of the bride or groom before the wedding, you have to treat it as a freebie and really control it. Because it's not the same as when they call you out of the blue and initiate a family portrait session. But it is definitely an area that can be very lucrative. So, if you manage it properly, you'll get extra sales. The idea behind giving a free session to the bride's and groom's families also gives you extra marketing ammunition when you're selling your wedding photography, because you can tell them, "Oh, and you can get this as well as a free bonus." So it's a free bonus idea and sales pitch.

THE ULTIMATE SALES PITCH

When I'm selling family portraits after the session's done, assuming that I've done everything else properly, it's pretty much a cakewalk. But I still want to do a good job. If I photograph an outdoor session, I've taken a lot of different angles and a lot of variety. I photograph not only the regular poses, but I try to photograph interactive poses. There are several reasons for this. One, they don't expect it. Two, the final proofing will go much, much better. And three, I can create a slide show with these images. It's pretty boring to create a slide show when it's just straight-on poses. But when you add a lot of interactive type poses to a family session, and create a slide show out of those proofs, and add music to it, wow, have you got something powerful with which to leverage your sales process.

I do this with every session that I photograph outdoors. And I create two slide shows – one is a proof show where it's just the proof numbers and they get to look at each group one at a time; and the other is a proof show set to music, and its sole purpose is to move them at a very deep and emotional level. So when my clients come back to the studio and they're there to see their final images, I treat it like a presentation. And I explain to them, "Okay, we're about to watch your images. And I've created two slide shows for you. The first one is really just for your entertainment. It's just something that I thought was kind of special, and it's set to music. So don't worry about looking at any of the images and deciding on any of them right away. We're going to get to that eventually." And then I run the show. Now don't forget, the music is set to surround sound with a sub-woofer, large screen or video projected and very, very dynamic. And the moms will cry. And the dads will open their wallets.

I should mention at this time as well, and this applies to virtually every session, one of the selling angles and tools that I use is something that I created out of observation and necessity. A lot of clients would ask me what the best pose, in my opinion, was. They would think, and maybe rightfully so or not, I'm not sure; they would think that I had some special skill or talent in spotting the perfect pose. But I don't know that I agree with that idea, because I really think that they know which is the best pose, because they know their family much more intimately. And the way they know is by using the explanation and technique as follows: I tell them before they look at a slide show or their proofs, "Look, a lot of people ask me this question – which are the best poses?"

"Well honestly, I don't know, but there is a rule of thumb that I like to use in order to get to the best poses. And that is this: When you're looking at your images and you instantly see an image that you like, when you have a gut reaction, that's your heart telling you that that image is very important to you. What happens all too often is the left side of your brain, the analytical side, will take over. Or maybe you'll be influenced by a well-meaning friend, or a sibling or a mother-in-law, who will come along and say, 'Well that's a nice image, but . . .'

"Don't listen to that but. Trust your heart and your first impression because if you instantly like an image, 20 years from now or 30 years from now, you're still going to love that image, and it'll have a lot of emotional value to you and a lot of meaning to you." So that's what I tell everybody. When they hear that, they really understand it. It makes a lot of sense, don't you think? And it really helps that selection process go a lot faster.

BEST TIME FOR FAMILIES

Is there a best time to photograph families? Some people ask me this. And I don't know that there is because life moves on. Life goes on all the time. Every year is a special time. So really there isn't a best time, in my opinion. Some people like to have a portrait done every year. Some people like to have them done every five years or every ten years. A lot of people wish they would have had them done more often. But there is no ideal time in any person's or family's life where you could have a family portrait. You will notice that a lot of family portraits will happen as children approach the age where they're leaving home, and a lot of moms will want to get that family photograph before the children leave home.

Anniversaries of course are another time – 40th, 50th, 25th anniversary. Wedding anniversaries are a good time to have those legacy portraits done, or when a family's very young – a new family. These are all different times that you could make a big deal out of, and use as marketing messages and marketing strategies. And you're, in effect, targeting these different groups and telling them, 'Look, this is an important time right now.'

Another important time is Christmas time. Every year you could sell a special with some cool little packages that you could use as, well you might want to call them loss leaders – you know where you sell an introductory offer, say $49 and it includes an 8x10 and 12 Christmas cards or sell that for $99 or $19.95. It depends on the volume. Where you set that price will determine the amount of volume that will come to your studio. And it all depends on where you are at, and where you want to grow to. But that's the general rule of thumb when you're creating specials that are time sensitive to seasons.

CHAPTER 14

Publicity

"The fight is won or lost far away from witnesses - behind the lines, in the gym, and out there on the road, long before I dance under those lights."

- Muhammad Ali
(Three time World Heavyweight Boxing
Champion and Olympic Gold Medalist)

A ds are not believable. Publicity is believable. People are reluctant when they see an ad. They immediately cast suspicion upon it. So that's why using direct response, benefit laden, and feature loaded advertising, with a specific time sensitive deadline and a dynamic offer, is important. Otherwise, you're really not doing your hard spent advertising dollars any justice by using anything less, than the most dynamic marketing strategies for your ads. But using publicity is even better. Why? Because it's believable. And the best part is it's free. The problem is, though, publicity takes a little bit of innovative and concerted effort on your part, and it takes more time. And it is a little less measurable in a sense that you don't have as much control over it. But it is very, very powerful and it is, above all, dirt cheap.

IMPORTANCE OF PUBLICITY

Why is publicity so effective? And why is it so believable? Well first of all, it comes from an objective source. If you were written about in your local newspaper, it's not you bragging about yourself. It's not you talking about yourself in your ad. It's somebody else – a neutral third party objective viewpoint, and they are saying all these wonderful things about you. Think about the many times that you were given a referral to go to a certain restaurant – a new restaurant in town – and you actually followed that advice. Or you heard about a new movie that was playing, and you went to see it, because of the positive reviews you heard from a friend or a trusted advisor. That's publicity! When your client leaves your studio, at the very basic level, publicity is working. This is also just as important, if not more important, than every other level of your marketing in your studio. When a client picks up their portrait at the very end and pays their balance, and they leave, everything that they say and all the interaction that goes on about the family portrait or whatever portrait, that goes on between them and their friends, is entirely, 100 percent all publicity.

That's why branding is so weak. When people use branding as an argument or a marketing strategy, I think it's utter nonsense. It's ridiculous. Branding is really publicity. But it's new terminology created by designers and advertising people to make it sound like this valuable new strategy called branding, and it is something that they should spend a fortune on in their ad. Branding, when you look at it in the true sense, is publicity. It is a brand; it is that impression that they have upon you, not through your advertising, but the experiences that have been conveyed from others, from an objective viewpoint. That's why publicity is so powerful.

That's why referral programs are so good in photography. When you hand out a card or several cards, and you give this to a happy client, and say, "Here. Give this to five of your closest friends, would you?" And they are cards that have great samples, or actual samples from that specific shoot, and it has their name on it and it says, 'Come in for a half-price portrait session or a free portrait session, or a portrait session and a free 8x10, or two free 5x7s, or whatever.' It matters not. When they give these cards out, they're handed to them from a source that is, for the most part, objective and neutral. They're just saying, "Look, go check out these guys. They're good. I used them. I trust them. And I would suggest that you do so as well.' This is publicity. That's actually publicity, working in an actual marketing strategy.

But if you want to get publicity in your community, you should really look at doing articles, television and radio media. And this requires a little bit more innovation. When you're creating publicity in your area and you want to get a journalist writing about you, you have to create a reason for them to want to write about you. And that reason should never be selfish, nor should it be about how wonderful your studio is. You have to find things of interest to their viewers or readers that they will want to write, or present to their viewers, because what you have to say is interesting.

You could be talking about trends in photography. You could be talking about different cameras. You could be talking about different areas in your town that are of photographic importance. You could talk about what is the more popular, and that is awards. And most newspapers will make mention of any major awards that you might win. You can write press releases, and you can use strategies in your press releases that will get results. But I would suggest that you not use boring, old, standard, run-of-the-mill press releases. Why not make your press releases stand out above the rest. Everything else should, shouldn't it? Create a two-page press release.

In my marketing system, I created a whole report, about 25 pages or so, dedicated to the creation of press releases. I don't have enough time to write about it in this book, I think you get the general idea that when you create a press release, you really ought to be using topics or suggestions that are of interest. That's really the gist of it. Page two of the press release is nothing more than a list of questions that the reporter could potentially ask you. This is really cool and the reason is because they never see this that often. And really what you're doing is you're making their job easier. So when you come up with some questions – and they may or may not use them or they might even use some of them and modify parts of the questions – the fact that you presented that to them; and let's assume you presented them a really good and attractive idea that they would potentially want to use as a news piece to their audience and then you've added these questions. And let's assume they're good questions, not selfish or narrowly defined questions. Let's also assume that you did all this properly; you will get noticed, when you send in this type of a press release.

You could also kind of cheat this a little bit; you could create your own articles and put an ad in. And of course you've seen those before – they're called advertorials. The newspapers always insist that you write 'advertisement' across the top or bottom. Make sure that when you do create these kinds of advertorials that you put the statement "advertisement" on the bottom. Use the very, smallest, possible script that you can, and use all caps. Use the skinniest font you can so it's not too perceptive. And it's amazing how many people reading this will think it's an article, and they'll even see the word, "advertisement." If you do this properly and it's informative, they will automatically associate it with a regular article and subconsciously or consciously, or both, think that it's a credible source. Why you know, it actually is if you've got a good product and good service, and you follow through on your promises, you are a good source. And you do have a good business, and you have good reason to extol the benefits of your services and products.

A MARKETING "POWER TOOL"

Publicity is a wonderful tool. And it's a great way to enhance the credibility and to make fast inroads if you're starting out in your community. I personally know photographers who have used this and have created much success because of their publicity efforts. But it does take a concerted and focused effort. The vast majority will not use publicity, let alone use it in an innovative way, so this gives you the advantage to use a rarely used strategy. Some photographers have effectively used it and received national, and regional, and local media attention, on an ongoing basis. And you could do the same, too.

If you use publicity and your local media, and you have a program where you are constantly sending in press releases, and you are sending in valuable and informative articles or suggestions for articles, you will get results, and you will be written about and talked about from very credible sources. What somebody says about you is infinitely far more powerful than what you say about yourself. That's why testimonials are such a powerful tool in all your marketing and why you should be using them all the time, especially testimonials that are results driven as opposed to testimonials that are so, so and just okay. We don't really want to use testimonials that say things like, "You were very, very, very, very adequate." Or you don't want testimonials that are vague, such as; "We had a great time at our wedding."

What you want to hear is testimonials like, "Rob, we had no idea that when we saw the pictures, it would make us react and cry and feel that we hired the right studio to capture our wedding photography. I was so stressed out on my wedding day, and you made it so much easier that I really appreciated you being there." See, those are results; those are specifics. Specifics in your testimonials are important. But I digress.

Even if the two are linked, there is enough evidence out there that point to the power of publicity as the strategy that has built and created virtually a lot of successful businesses. A lot of people think that it's the national advertising. But really, the national advertising that is spent on a lot of these large companies is nothing more than maintenance, or an attempt at maintenance, which really ends up being a waste of money, considering the stupidity and shallowness of most ads. But when you look at how most businesses evolve in their start-up phases of life, publicity played a very, very important role.

Publicity plays a very important role in the development of a lot of events and businesses that we witness all the time. It is the underlying foundational truth that is all too often ignored as the momentum and the progression that made the business congeal and grow, and which created a brand in the minds of the local people, which is what it is for us photographers – we really should not be too obsessed or concerned with national or even regional advertising or publicity, for that matter.

Websites

I drive a motorcycle. It's one of my favourite activities. I'm not a speed demon or anything of that nature, by any stretch of the imagination, but I do enjoy a finely tuned machine. And I'm very capable when it comes to riding. However, like a lot of things in life, I want to know as much as possible about the risks and some of the inherent dangers. So when I got my latest motorcycle, one of the things that I did was I went onto Google®, and I searched 'high speed wobble.' A high-speed wobble is a risk that can happen with just about any motorcycle, however I wanted to know a little more about it because I wanted to inform myself of this risk. Similarly, when my wife travels – and that's something we do quite a bit – she also uses Google® and various other website portals to do a lot of research. Why am I telling you this stuff? It's a fact of life. The web is a daily occurrence and a source of information for just about every home and family in the free world. And it is something that we can be using in our studios if we use the right strategies and the right techniques.

It occurred to me many, many years ago when the web was just starting out, somewhere in the mid to latter part of the 1990s, that the web would be a great place to get information to people. And it would be an ideal place for studios. I envisioned in my mind, a typical prospect of mine, either a bride or a mom who's thinking about having a family portrait done. I would envision her in her home, in the privacy of her own room, where she was able to go and do research without feeling pressured. And that she could just go out and do as much of this on her own, at her own pace that she desired. And that this would be a natural activity that would resonate with most of the prospects that come into my studio. I think I'm fairly close to describing the picture that reflects reality.

WOMEN AND THE WEB

Most women, and they happen to be the majority of my clients, and probably are the majority of yours, if you're running a portrait and wedding studio, like to go and find information on the web. It is something that they enjoy doing, but the frustrating part can be, but that is easily resolved, is the lack of good, useful, information. Most websites do a very poor job, in my opinion, at giving the right information. As a photographer, you can use the web to get information into your prospects' hands. Now, your website and use of the Internet should be to inform – to inform prospects, and to inform clients. Plus it also can be used in, and should be used as, a lead generation tool. So there's a two-pronged approach to using the web. And I want to talk a little bit about both.

Using information comes in the form of, obviously, putting a lot of samples on your site. Now it is my opinion that you should be putting as many and as much variety as is possible, and getting that information to your prospects as quickly as possible. That's why I don't like using slide shows or any kind of complex web gallery where they have to click on each image, one at a time. I like to use small images, where I can load many on a page. And I also like to support the images with a lot of copy, good copy, and copy that pitches offers and copy that pitches a call to action, and also drives them to the studio, either via e-mail, telephone, or a sign-up for a newsletter that informs. That's using the web as a lead generation tool. You can use it to take visitors, and bring them into your studio, and turn them into clients.

THE HUNT FOR GOOD PHOTOGRAPHERS

There is a way to determine how many people, on any average month, are searching for photographers in your area on the web. It's easily discovered how many people might be typing in certain terms or a variety of search terms. All you have to do is pick your area. Start with your city, or if you're in a larger city, you could search in a section of the city. Or you could open it up into either a state or province, and type in 'photographer' or 'photography' or 'photography studio' with those terms. And you can easily find out by going through some of the web optimization tools that are available out there, and you could discover how many times, on average per month, people are actually looking for a photographer in your area.

This is valuable information. And I've discovered there are quite a few in my area, and it surprises me that so few studios know this information or capitalize on it. It is good information to know because you can tap into these searches and these people who are searching and drive them to your site, because obviously they are searching for a photographer for a reason. That makes them hot leads. That makes them hot prospects. So you can drive that traffic to your website by using basic search optimization techniques. Now I don't have enough room, or time, to get into all of the specifics, but it's easily discoverable. It's out there. It's almost become common knowledge. And if you take advantage of these techniques, and apply them into your studio website, you can easily get a certain amount of business.

Now I wouldn't rely on a website 100 percent, but it is a dimension of your marketing that you should be using as a lead generation tool. Also to get leads and or traffic to your site, you could use direct ads in local media or in any piece of marketing that you do, either through postcards, business cards, displays, newspaper ads, or classified ads. You can drive people locally to your website and then continue the sales message from there.

A WEBSITE IS MORE THAN AN ELECTRONIC BILLBOARD

To use your website as an information tool is the other area that is of big benefit. You could not only put a lot of samples, and categorize your samples, so that you can niche the different areas for babies, for children, children of different age groups, families, families of different categories, or weddings, but you could do commercial photography. You could niche it in any way, shape or form that you want. You could devote a whole page to a certain area in your town that is renowned for its backdrops, and maybe it has scenic value for photographs.

There are many ways that you could creatively carve up your website into interesting little dimensions that will be of benefit to the local people who go and visit it. You could have a page dedicated just to new samples from the last few months. And that will drive people back to your website, because a lot of people, especially a lot of women, always like to see what's new, what's exciting, what's recent, what's cool. Your website could include pages of portrait preparation tips, which are really there to help create a better product for your clients and prospects, therefore assisting you in the sales process.

You could have a monthly newsletter. That's something I do in my studio. Sign up. Every month I get sign-ups for my newsletter. And the newsletter is really simple. Because they're asking to be a part of the newsletter, now I have permission to send them an email. And of course I wouldn't abuse that privilege, but now I am able to send them a monthly newsletter at the very least. And the newsletter is nothing more than some useful information on photography, some useful information on some specials; maybe I can offer them exclusive specials. I can also show them recent samples and ideas, or anything new. I can even talk about the same ideas that I would talk about in my printed newsletters that are non-photography related, but have a local and community flavour. As long as it's interesting and new, and written in a conversational style, I can really intensify the email communications. And I do so with permission from them.

BE SURE TO MAINTAIN CONTROL

The worst person in my opinion to take control of your website is a web designer or a graphic designer. Let me underscore that by making it clear that a webmaster will have a useful purpose. But what you don't want a webmaster to do is to take complete control and complete charge of your marketing on the web. The idea here is that you are in charge of content and direction, and they are there to pull together the technical side of things. And you have to make it very clear. Because honestly, what does a graphic designer or a webmaster know about selling portraits? Is it something they do, day in and day out? Of course not. They do designs and technical stuff to do with the web. You are the best salesperson for your photography, so you should be in charge of the content and the direction of your website. You should use a website because it is so cheap, and so easy and flexible. And if you are ambitious, you could actually learn the very basics of web design. It is so simple.

I work at my web design, and I designed my site all by myself, just by following some very basic, fundamental rules. My website is clean and lean, and uncluttered. And I can change samples on an ongoing basis. And if you go to it, you'll see what I mean. It's www.westmount-photography.com You'll see what I mean, how on the first page it loads very fast, and there are different categories. And there's also always a bit of news or something recent and newsy, and perhaps a pitch or an offer, and different categories on the different styles of photography that I do. I believe in, again, using a lot of photographs, so all the different categories on my main page are represented by photographs. And they are rollover photographs, too. So when the mouse is placed on top of it, they see a second image. There's also a picture of me. I believe it's important to use you and your personality as the driving force behind all of your marketing. So, why not put a picture of yourself. Talk a little bit about yourself on your website.

KEY WEBSITE MISTAKES

Some of the common mistakes I see in web design are things like not changing the data. It's old and stale, and it kind of gets forgotten about. Or they don't know how to optimize their site for search engines. Or they don't do search term research and look into web search terms that are being sought after, and how that can effectively create a great deal of flow and leads to your website.

Another big mistake, in my opinion, is the use of slide shows and music on the website. This seems to be very popular with a lot of photographers, and I don't think it helps matters. And there are several reasons why I believe this. First of all, it's slow. Most people don't have patience to sit around and wait. The idea behind this is that it's cool and it's entertaining. But I really don't think that entertainment, in this respect, is going to increase the sales process. People want to get the information, and they want it now. They don't want to be entertained, and listen to music and watch effects, while they're getting to that information. So, for many, it's an ego thing. It's a photographer's vanity. And a lot of photographers feel that it's important that they have these slide shows, and they're doing them for the wrong reason, in my opinion. Another reason why I think a slide show is a bad idea is, it's very technical. Well, maybe it's not. I'm not sure, but it's way beyond me. So, I like to keep things simple. When I go to my website, I can do just about any change I want to; fast and easy. It's ridiculously simple. However, if I had a slide show or one of those Flash shows, I wouldn't know the first thing about how they're created online, nor do I have the desire or the inclination to want to learn how to do that, because I just will never be using slide shows on my site; not in that respect.

Now, I do use and show slide shows, but not in the way that is commonly used in a lot of websites, where you go to the site and the first thing that pops up is a slide show. That's not the way I believe a slide show should be used. The way I use slide shows is I link from the page, and it's usually somewhere in the middle of one of the categories. Say for example, child portraiture on the child portrait page, somewhere about a third of the way down on the second page where I've loaded it with more information, more copy, more text, and more calls to action, there's a link that says, 'Click here and you can watch a slide show.' And it's a compilation of images, and it opens up in a separate browser so that they can keep going back to the original browser. And if they want to, they can keep looking at it and reading it. But at least they have the option of watching that if they want, or they can click it off if it loads too slowly for them, or if they're not patient enough. So I do use slide shows in that respect. I also have a slide show of all my favourite wedding images from the year before – I call it the Showcase. And it is linked from an email that they receive when they request information.

WEB WORK – THE RIGHT WAY

I use emails quite effectively and quite a bit in my studio and on several different venues. First of all, if anybody goes to my website and they want to get prices, they can have the prices, but they've got to send me an email, and it's an auto-responder. And the email they get from me is a sales pitch, obviously; but it's got links to sales letters and information packets and slide shows, and a call to action, of course, to the studio. All of this is designed to get people to try and call the studio. So when they get an email, it will have a link to the slide show Showcase; to the wedding photography. For the regular prices and portrait prices, I'll also have slide shows linked in the email as well, even though they are already off the website itself. It's a good thing to recycle this stuff and have it promoted as many times, and in as many places, including emails, as is possible.

The information that I use via the web is quite extensive. I have the

PDF booklet that I created, and the price list is a multi-page booklet with a load of information in it. I also have a portrait tips booklet; it's about 13-14 pages long. And likewise for weddings, I have a report; it's about 14 pages long – it's called '7 *Mistakes Brides Make When Hiring a Professional Wedding Photographer and What You Can Do to Avoid Them.*' And of course, my wedding price list is also as long, or longer. And the reason that I have these long form, multi-page, letters is because I want to get a lot of information, and I want to describe everything and explain everything, so that everybody knows what it is that I'm trying to say about my products and services.

Also as an aside, when you use these techniques, because hardly anybody uses them, you stand out above the rest. You look like a hero. You look like somebody who cares and somebody who is willing to go the extra mile by putting together all this extra information for your prospects. The web is a great way to get this data, and it is becoming so common place for people to access information, to access it quickly, and in web form via email, PDF form, online slide shows, and what not.

KNOW YOUR CLIENTELE

But it's important to keep in mind that you have to stay in touch with basic human behaviours. Know what is going on in your client's mind. How are they thinking? What is the conversation that's going on in their heads? When they slide up to the computer, and she's serious about getting a family portrait done, and she happens to know your website. What is she anticipating? What kind of information is she looking for? What questions does she have in her head that she either knows or questions that she doesn't know she knows, but they're there anyway, floating around in her subconscious just behind her consciousness.

Pre-emptively ask and answer as many of these questions and include that information on your website. It baffles me to no end why photographers don't get this. Probably, it has a lot to do with what I call marketing incest. Marketing incest is when a lot of people in the same industry all get together at conferences and conventions, and they all start to share notes and look at what the other guy is doing. And they start to copy what the other guy is doing when they go home. And this happens after so many years, that it ends up being real stupid and dumb, and totally ineffective. And the initial premise barely had an ounce of credibility to it. So by the time it's evolved, it's even more watered down and sterile. And stupid.

So it's important to step outside of our industry, and step outside the box, and push the envelope, and look at new and innovative ways to use our website to get the information on a real level with our prospects and clients, and get into their hearts and souls and minds, and use this media, which is such a powerful and accessible need for all of us to take advantage of. Let's get away from the photographer's vanity. Let's put our egos aside and look at what really matters here. The black background, white text, which happens to be one of the hardest combinations to read, may massage our ego and make us feel like we're doing something that looks really cool. But will a prospect look at that and go, "Ooooh. Wow. I like that. That looks nice. That white text on the black background makes me want to buy portraits." So keep it simple, keep it clean, keep it lean and mean. And make your website work and work hard for you. It's so easy to do. All we have to do is get it right.

CHAPTER 16

Dictate or Be Dictated To

"I want to put a ding in the universe."

- Steve Jobs
(Co-founder and CEO of Apple)

Lies, lies, lies. Let's talk about lies . . .

I've noticed at many seminars, where a photographer tries to pull a rabbit out of his hat, or pull out some obscure sounding, almost magical formulaic solution or complex law of physics, that just confounds everybody. And every time I hear this, I think to myself, what a load. Geez, lighten up.

Examples like "wrap-around lighting", or using logos, or "branding", or the idea that talent is "God-given", that you are either born with it and it is some divine right, or you just are not. I mean, this is nothing but pure and utter nonsense. And on . . . the lies continue. Don't fall for them. Know the difference and at least know what to ignore. That way you get to create your own destiny.

What does it take to succeed? And how long does it take to succeed? It's a very simple formula. It's nothing more than a matter of time, desire, and, of course, the willingness to be a good student. You don't have to be an exceptional photographer, although I believe in time that you will develop a sense of mastery. If you look at any photographer who's been doing this for most of his or her life, like some of the older masters in their 70s, they have been doing it so long that it is almost a Zen-like confidence with an ability to create the outstanding images virtually effortlessly.

Mind you, their styles may not have changed a whole lot, but that doesn't matter. They're doing quality work; probably a lot better than what many of us are doing right now in our lives, and in our studios. But what I can't stand is when some arrogant fool comes along and says, 'Well you're either born with it, or you're not.' That's a load of crap. Listen, you can get good at anything. It's no different than playing a musical instrument.

I always like to compare musicians and musical instruments when I'm talking about photography and developing your skills. And this includes marketing as well, because when you're, say for example, a guitar player and you're trying to learn a song, you can do it with enough practice.

But the guitar players that really seem to excel are the ones that know a little bit more about marketing. They are probably better guitar players than most of the guitar players in the top bands today.

For the sake of argument, we'll talk about Keith Richards, an old-timer; classic rocker from the Rolling Stones. He was the first one to admit that he's not a great guitar player.

There are many far, far superior to him, but he's the one that's willing to get out there with the Rolling Stones, who are master marketers, they get out there and put on a show. Give the people what they want. It's all about the "putting on the show", not the quality of the playing, given the fact that the quality is still a certain level. In other words, it's marketing. So being able to put on a show, as well as handling the business side of things, is equally as important as knowing how to take care of the technical side of things. But anybody could do it with enough time, persistence, and skill. It's not a gift that you're born with. Give me a break.

You have eyes, and you have the desire to learn how light and composition work, and how people desire nice looking photographs, and you're not afraid to sell, and if you have the confidence to grow your business, then you can be a success.

Don't let anybody dictate to you what the rules of the game are. You get to decide what the rules of the game are. And you get to decide how far it is you want to go and how fast you want to get there. Don't let external influences, either through association or individuals, or people that you look up to, tell you otherwise.

GUILTY BY ASSOCIATION

Associations are pretty guilty at times of keeping people back. Naively we let it happen to ourselves. A lot of people join associations, and they are wonderful resources, don't get me wrong. I love going to all my associations. I attend as many conferences and conventions as are possible. And I love the camaraderie and the friendship, and all the events and seminars, and print competitions. But there's often the inner politics, and bull crap that goes along with it that complicates things and sidetracks issues. And really, their attempt is to try and keep people in the dark, either on an individual level or through committees and/or board of directors. Most of these cases are nothing more than frustrated individuals, fearful of your success, jealous that you are successful, and either not able to succeed themselves for whatever reason, letting their frustration manifest itself by controlling others through mandates, by-laws, rules and whatever else the committee or position they belong to allows them to control. It's sad, but an inevitable reality.

Fortunately we can recognize, bypass, and tolerate the game, and know our own priorities, as long as we are aware and focused. You are in charge of your own destiny: you get to decide and you get to dictate. Not by some committee or sense of self-worth derived from belonging to one.

HOCUS POCUS

Anytime there sounds like a magical formula to either becoming a better photographer or becoming a better marketer, it isn't so. There isn't any magic to it. It's all an illusion.

The fact is that it takes work, discipline, persistence, and a willingness to learn from your mistakes and hardships, so that when really bad things happen to you, you just get back up and keep going. And you stay focused on the big goal. The big goal is your big vision, your five-year plan, your one-year plan, and your one-month plan. What are you going to do today? Next week? So when a photographer or an instructor pulls out some of these cool sounding strategies that are nothing more than rabbits out of a hat, second guess them. It's nonsense. We can get caught up in the technical side of things thinking that there are many methodologies and/or systems for us that are secret, unknown, magical and mysterious. Get away from that thinking and look at what's real. Look at what you are capable of doing. Look at what's important to you.

For example: Wrap around light. One that I hear from speakers is this terminology called wrap around light, like as if it is some special kind of lighting technique. Well, last I heard and when I was in college for all of what, 45 minutes, was that light – and this was taught in physics class – light travels in a straight line. It didn't bend, wrap around, curve or do anything of that nature. It just went in a straight line, and if it hit an object, it would bounce off in an equal angle to whatever angle that was coming in off that object. That's it. That's all. So what's this with wrap around lighting? I can't stand it when instructors do that, because it just sounds like they're trying to sound all mysterious and create these secretive, formulaic systems. Well, light doesn't wrap around. Let's not call it that. Let's just call "wrap around what it is – a large, soft light source".

Directional lighting; there's another one. Last I heard, all light was going in a direction. What is there? Directional lighting and non-directional lighting? Come on folks. All light is directional. So why are you calling it directional lighting?

Logos. There's another one that I can't stand. Advertising agencies and graphic designers are notorious for promoting the use of logos. These expensive and useless – I don't even want to call them marketing strategies, because they don't even fit in the realm of market strategies – are nothing more than a waste of money. Okay, if you really insist that you've got to get a logo, at least keep it simple and don't spend all your life savings on it. There's nothing magical, mysterious . . . and I don't care what your argument is, I've heard them all. This whole idea of branding and creating something in the minds of your subject and your prospects, in my opinion, bottom line, is nothing more than a load, nothing more than an illusion – another rabbit out of the hat.

If you want to create positive, memorable memories for your prospects, read the chapter on publicity. What your clients say about you is far more important than what a logo will say about you.

EXECUTIVES, ROTARIANS AND OTHER FAT CATS

In 1998, I joined the local Rotary International®. I was intimidated to say the least, but someone recently had told me a timely word of advice. He said something like: "Most executives and presidents, vice-presidents, wealthy people, etc., are no different, no better, no worse, than you. Unless of course their actions say otherwise." The main point was not to put others who are of status on a pedestal. This hit me hard. Woke me up. It made so much sense that it affected me to this day. I would have, in a prior lifetime, been intimidated by many of these folks. Local bigwigs, politicians, even the chief of police (I'll never forget sitting next to the chief at one of our lunch meetings, thinking to myself that not so long ago I was a client of his – cuffs and all – well, I've come a long way since my brief yet troubled teen years – before photography). From that moment on I never let another person sway me. Their status or otherwise was meaningless. Who they were on the inside mattered, and I developed the ability to relate to others at this level. It was, and is, one of the landmarks in my life. Very exhilarating and freeing. Maybe it helped, maybe it didn't. I believe it did. It brought me up to a level where I could relate to others, no matter who they were or stood for. My advice to you is never let anyone try and intimidate you or allow yourself to be intimidated, by others. Besides, you want to stay focused and do a great job when you photograph all these people.

BRASS BALLS – GET SOME

Success is a very personal matter – just like religion, politics and sex. However, we let people influence us, bend us or otherwise assault us with their opinions that all too often lead us down the wrong path.

If you want to succeed and be the best you can be – after all, being successful in your photography business is a natural part of "growing" and "self-actualization" – then developing a strong sense of self and self-confidence, and doing what you need to do to achieve this state on an ongoing basis, is key. I tell people, especially young people just starting out: Don't take advice from your parents. Also, never take advice from the camera store guy. I mean really, what do they know? Your mom loves you way too much. You can do no wrong in her eyes; all your images are awesome as far as she is concerned. The camera store guy – well, what's he doing selling cameras if he knows so much about running a successful photography studio?

This includes your peers and close friends. I heard a cool formula and I believe it to be true. Take your ten closest friends, total their net worth, divide that amount by ten, and that will be your net worth. It's one way of saying there is a self-imposed glass ceiling. The solution?

Know when to be strong, and turn away from, and repel against, anyone else's opinions, especially when it has the potential to do damage. Knowing when, and knowing who, and bringing this confidence with us throughout our entire lives, is part of having the proverbial "brass balls". It is the key to success.

THE LOST ART – COMMUNICATING THROUGH WORDS

No matter how words come at us, they are one of the most powerful tools. Be it the spoken word, reading, music or movies – words have a very, very strong impact on our brains. This will never change, even in spite of huge leaps and progress in technology. The way humans perceive, take in and paint huge emotional and visual images in our minds, because of the words used, will always be a part of our make up. Therefore, it's a good thing to understand this, and use it to our benefit. We can and should master the use of words in all of our communication – during shoots, in our ads and marketing, our presence in the studio, if we are giving any sort of presentation – whatever. It is an essential tool that we could all use to help us in our photography and in our business.

WHY I LOVE MONDAYS – TWO REASONS

I love Mondays because I just had Sunday off. And Sunday is a total do nothing day. I feel refreshed because of this. I also love Mondays because, even though I do end up being productive, I have no actual agenda.

But, the second and most important reason why I love Mondays is because I love my "job" (not really a job in the way most jobs are perceived sense), and Monday is the start of a new week.

LIVE & WORK BY DESIGN – YOURS!

Living is scary. Making money is scary. Doing your own thing is scary. It's all about responsibility, ultimately. But equally, even though responsibility sounds restraining, it isn't; it's really all about being free. The added responsibility means we have to make decisions – our decisions. Not the decisions of others.

Yes, we may screw up. We may stumble. We may even stumble real bad and real hard. But if you want to design your own life and live on your own terms, you have to tune out the rest of the world. All the messages, the noise, inner and outer, and listen to ourselves. And act.

This is scary. But do it anyways. Hey, look at me. I'm naked on he cover of my first book.

COMPETITION

Is competition a good thing? Absolutely. It makes you a better person, photographer and business person. When you look at your competition in business, you can react one of two ways; throw in the towel and blame the "market", or force yourself to create better solutions. Either way, the winner is the client. They don't want to hear you whine and complain, and certainly won't benefit by the lower level work that that attitude creates, so you may as well leave.

If you decide to take the harder path, the path of most resistance, your client wins because you create better images and better solutions. Competition forces the best from us. Any outside force that suppresses it should be removed.

If you happen to be in a competition free zone, you aren't doing yourself or your clients a favour. What will you do if after years of riding that gravy train things change and all you ever knew was easy business? Most wouldn't know what to do because that part never got trained in them. One of the worst things is having too much money. Throwing money at a situation isn't always wise. Too often it's the easy way out (until all the money's gone) and we're better off working out creative solutions without money.

Then there's print competitions. One thing about print competitions, and it's the same in any industry, is they do not reflect reality. Most images in a print show are not sellable. They do not, generally speaking, reflect the marketplace. There are some exceptions, but they are rare, and I'm not out to diss them. There are good reasons to compete in them, but you need to keep it in perspective. I shouldn't have been, but was in shock when a pet show photographer told me that many families are devastated and ruined over dog shows. It shouldn't have surprised me. It likely happens in many areas, especially when dealing with shows that involve pets, or people, like those beauty pageants for very young girls.

As photographers we need to guard against making print competitions the end all and be all. The main benefit in my opinion is they can make you a better photographer. That, again, is the main purpose of competing, in business or in shows.

Of course it's nice to bring home a few ribbons and accolades, but if we become obsessed and fail in other more important areas, like building a business, then it becomes nothing more than a neurotic impulse hopelessly trying to fill a shallow empty ego or an all out addiction that could leave us without much conscious.

Print competitions are fun competitions. And they should stay that way, as they show us to better our craft so we can apply the finer elements thereof and apply that where it matters most; in our product. So ultimately, it's about creating a better service and product for our clients. How can a print show judge ever quantify that?

THE ULTIMATE FORM OF COMPETITION

Competition is at the very root of all innovation. During the two world wars there was massive amounts of technological innovation because of the life or death competition that was forced upon humans during war. But there is a much better way to compete and innovate so everyone wins. Compete against yourself.

When you create a must-do drive and desire, and a clear vision of where you want to go, you are competing against yourself. Problem is, if you loose, you loose, and only you loose. But the bigger problem is, you have no one to be accountable to, so loosing ain't that bad. Here in lies the nugget of truth. Be aware of this fact and you gain a competitive edge over yourself and everyone else. Be accountable, to you. When you do, and you succeed, you win and everyone wins. Know that, and act in spite of lack of accountability, and you rise above the rest. Fact is most business owners have no plan. Or, they have ideas bouncing around in their heads, but no clear cut goals and plans on how to achieve them. When you have a plan, a set of goals and a vision, and you take steps, as many steps as you possibly can with what resources and time you have, then you are on your way. You win. That's competition.

FINALLY: THE SECRET TO SUCCESS

It's not about lighting, cameras or props. It goes much, much deeper. Would you like to know how to succeed? It's simple really; all you have to do is succeed. Really. Once you succeed once, even just a little but, you attract more success.

It's like magic and very powerful. Ah, but how do you succeed in the first place you ask? How can you get success if you ain't got none? Okay, that's a fair question and it certainly sounds like a catch-22 doesn't it. In order to create success out of thin air you must start with a vision, an idea, a goal, a clear mental picture of what it is you see yourself succeeding at. You must convince yourself of this on an hourly, daily, weekly and monthly basis. Without this you are wandering aimlessly.

At your deepest unconscious level you have a success barometer. It tells you how well you will do. It's like a ladder with only so many rungs on it. Everyone has their own unique barometer and we are limited by the possibilities this sets for us. Why are so many people stuck earning $40,000.00 a year, year after year? It's their internal success barometer.

This barometer controls us, and if we head for any opportunity or success it will pull us back, drag us down. So how do we get over any limits our own barometers may have placed on our own destiny? By using our imaginations we can slowly increase the level of our own barometer. It takes work but it will have an effect, and when opportunities come your way you will be able to take advantage of them instead of sabotaging them. You must imagine what it will be like to be in that place that you call success. Remember, get a clear mental picture.

Other ways to work your barometer is by doing the very things that scare you. Fear is paralyzing. It serves no useful purpose other than killing your dreams, or telling to not put your hand on a red hot stove. Now you don't have to be logical about this, go after any fear. When you confront them you grow. It increases your inner barometer overall.

Seems simple doesn't it? But we choose to stay stuck and let our fears hold us back. What about talents? You may feel you lack certain skills or pre-dispositions. Or worse yet you bought into the biggest lie, that you had be born with talent. This I am happy to report to you is one of the biggest lies ever uttered by pompous, never-well-meaning and arrogant misguided souls. It's used by these poor, self absorbed windbags to try and push you down and hold you back. Don't buy it for a second.

I will concede that people are born with certain pre-dispositions, such as body types that may be suitable for athletics, and if you are born blind you may never take up career as a pilot, but these are the exceptions to the rule. Even so, many people have accomplished incredible feats in spite of serious setbacks. The idea that you are born a certain way is preposterous. It's a load of crap whose time has come to an end. You can do and be anything you want.

You get good at something by getting good. It's that simple. It takes work. That's why so many hang their hat on the "I-wasn't-born-with-it excuse". They're lazy. Everybody wants to be rich or famous but few are willing to do whatever is necessary to get there.

If you want to learn or enhance a new skill start it now, and learn it every day, day after day and you will get good. Keep learning new things. It's good for the brain. It keeps you young and vibrant. When you learn new things don't give up because it seems hard at first.

Every new skill, new passage has the same basic steps it must follow. First, unconscious incompetence, where you suck at it and you don't even know you suck at it. Conscious competence, where you suck at it but at least you know you suck at it. Conscious competence, where you are good at it and you know it, you have to make conscious effort to maintain that level of being good at it, and finally, unconscious competence, mastery, where you seem to have that natural talent.

It just flows. This is where others will tell you that you are born with it. Like as if it was that easy.

Another one of the great, often ignored success principles is that of total responsibility. Always take the position that everything that happens in your life is all your fault. No, I'm serious on this. This will keep you sharp and in the right mindset, never defaulting to blaming.

So success seems to happen to others. On the outside this may certainly seem so, but if we look deeper we will find years of struggle and effort,and always a vision. If you want to succeed you must have your own vision. If you offer up excuses you're being a pessimistic, negative cry baby and nobody likes a cry baby. If you see success in someone else ask them how they did it, and listen, I mean really listen. There's gold in the answers. Likewise, never take advice from anyone who hasn't been there.

Done

"It's not that I'm smart, I just keep trying stuff until I get it right. Enhancing, or "fixing", requires that all the fundamentals of good photography be there – light, exposure, composition . . ."

- James Hodgins
(Photographer of the Year 2002, 2004,
and 2005, PPO North Eastern Branch)

This book is finished. I certainly hope you enjoyed it and perhaps got something out of it. I wasn't after any awards when I wrote it, certainly not any literary awards. I am a businessman who uses photography as his main craft for earning money. Photography is at the same time a serious passion and a whole lot of fun. I wouldn't have it any other way.

Let me finish with a few quotes that I have pasted by my desk.

"Most people waste their entire lives trying desperately to "get out of" or avoid exactly what is required for success and happiness."

- Dan Kennedy

"You are what you think."

- unknown

"The mind is always sharpest when there is a hanging at dawn."

- unknown

"YCDBSOYA"

(you can't do business sitting on your ass)

- Dan Kennedy

"Never take advice from anyone who hasn't been there."

- Me

"In a whirlwind of technological advances nothing seems to ever stay the same. Truth is, the fundamentals of good photography will never change.

Creating a dramatic image will always depend on the insight, planning and ability of the photographer to recreate what he or she sees in his or her mind and heart."

- Robert Provencher

Books and Websites I Recommend

SUCCESS TITLES

Think & Grow Rich - Napolean Hill (A must read, although a little dry and dated in it's style, the core message is excellent.)

The Magic of Believing - Claude Bristol

The Power of Your Subconscious Mind - Joseph Murphy

Profiles of Power and Success - Gene Landrum

Jump In - Mark Burnett

Made in America - Sam Walton

Learned Optimism - Martin Seligma

Thick Face, Black Heart - Chin Ming Chue

Looking Out for Number One - Robert Ringer

Anything by Dan Kennedy – search his name on Amazon and buy all his business books.

ECONOMICS TITLES

The Mystery of Capital - Hernando De Soto

Adventure Capitalist - Jim Rogers

MARKETING TITLES

Tested Advertising Methods - John Caples

My Life in Advertising/Scientific Advertising - Claude Hopkins
(Likely, the "bible" of all marketing/advertising books.)

Predatory Marketing - C. Britt Beemer

Method Marketing - Denny Hatch

The Invisible Touch - Harry Beckwith

Ogilvie on Advertising - David Ogilvie

The Fall of Advertising and Rise of PR - Al & Laura Ries

INFLUENCE: The Psychology of Persuasion - Robert Cialdini

OTHER TITLES

Blink and The Tipping Point - Malcolm Gladwell

Often Wrong, Never in Doubt - Donny Deutsch

The E Myth - Micheal Gerber

Freakonomics - Steven Levitt & Stephen Dubner

There are many more books that I have not mentioned here, but these are a few notables.

A COUPLE WEBSITES

Of course there are hundreds I could list, but these are most notable for the content.

www.NoBsPhotoSuccess.com

If you are not a member and you need to stay on top of some great photography tutorials, tips and digital news, then this is the place for you. It's like a one-stop community and complete resource center for the portrait and wedding photographer. Email us (I founded this site with co-founder James Hodgins) for a special sign-in discount. Tell us you read about it in this book.

www.ProfitableStudio.com

Dedicated to photography marketing. This is my site. I also put out a free, timely, monthly newsletter and the old newsletters are all archived. Also there are success systems for baby photography, wedding photography and marketing.

www.ScienceOfGettingRich.net

Money is not evil. Getting some, plenty of it, is part of your duty, responsibility and evolution. This is a must check out site. Get the manual (it's free) and buy the CD's.

www.TheGaryHalbertLetter.com

Loaded with all his free newsletters from years ago. Gary is considered to be the best marketer alive.

www.GapingVoid.com

This guy is cool, and fun. I love his book-in-progress on creativity. Click the link on the right that says: The most read page on Gaping Void is, How to be Creative. It's amazing.

The Author

Rob Provencher is a full-time professional photographer, and with the help of his wife Tina, continues to run a highly successful studio in a small remote town of only 90,000 people; and has done so for over 25 years.

In 2000 he received his Masters of Photographic Arts with the Professional Photographers of Canada and has earned over 20 National Merits and one loan collection. He is accredited in Wedding Photojournalism, Wedding Story, Environmental Wedding categories with the PPC and was Photographer of the Year in 1992, 1993 and 1995 in his area.

He co-creator of the *No BS Photo Success Online Forum* and teaches workshops all over North America, throughout the year, and has become known in the industry for his insightful, no-nonsense approach to success in marketing, posing, lighting and other key areas of success.

Rob is also the co-creator of the *Profitable Studio Marketing Success System, Freestyle Wedding Success System* and the *Baby and Children Photography Success* DVD series.

In addition to photography Rob has been active in Toastmasters since 1991 and earned ATM GOLD in 2002.

Robert Provencher, MPA

Index

If You Want to Take Your Digital Images up a Notch or Two, Try Craig's Actions

"The best set of commercially available Photoshop Actions I've ever used"

— Shutterbug Magazine

About Craig Minielly, founder of Craig's Actions:

Recognized as a leader in Commercial, Portrait, Industrial and Editorial assignments, he is also one of the pioneers of making successful use of Digital Techniques in a working studio.

Craig's Actions are some of the best on the market today. A must-have for the serious & dedicated pro portrait or commercial photographer. His techniques and applications are refined from years, decades of solid photographic experience, working with some of the most demanding and exacting clients. Craig's actions and his track record speak for themselves. Do yourself a huge favour!

no
BS
photo success

**"If Making More Money In
Your Photography Business And
Mastering Digital Photography
Is A Top Priority......."**

Sign Up With the Inner Circle Forum and Get Instant Access to Hundreds Of Kick-Butt Tutorials and Digital Photography Success Tools....

Discover why this place could very well be the best place for improving your photography, making more money marketing your photography business and sky rocketing your photographic skills.

There are not too many places where you can find this much information at your fingertips.

It's more like a BIG, GIANT SUPER-MEGA conference and online workshop.

Read more about the Inner Circle Members Forum at

www.NoBSPhotoSuccess.com

Printed in the United States
73874LV00003B/79-81